Confessions of a Prodigal Daughter

Revised Edition

SARAHBETH CAPLIN

Copyright © 2014 Sarahbeth Caplin

Cover design by Amy Queau, image from Shutterstock

All rights reserved.

ISBN-13: 978-1500563134

"If I am not, may God put me there; and if I am, may God so keep me."
-Joan of Arc's famous response to the trick question of whether she was in God's grace

Preface

Sitting in a hotel room in Jerusalem, I am facing my family, and they are waiting for me to come clean about a secret I've been hiding for almost a year. This is it, *I think to myself.* They know. *I have prayed for the strength to handle this moment in a mature, reasonable way, but now I have no words...*

Of all the New Testament parables I've read, the tale of the prodigal son beginning in Luke 15:11 resonates the most with me. It is the story of a man with two sons. The older of the two demanded his share of his father's inheritance before he died. The father agreed to divide his wealth evenly between them. The oldest continued to work for his father, but the younger son chose to squander his share on lavish, irresponsible living.

When he eventually ran out and began to starve, he came back to his father's house and asked to be taken in once again. Rather than demand an apology or explanation for his whereabouts, the father threw a party to celebrate his return. The older son chastised his father's decision to celebrate the return of his selfish brother, but the father said the occasion was worth celebrating, because "he once was lost, but now he has been found."

I've been the black sheep of my family for as long as I can remember. While my mother, father, brother and I all share the same dark, curly hair, blue-green eyes and dry sense of humor, our religious and political beliefs could not be more different. I grew up in a family that embraces cultural Judaism over spiritual Judaism. Everything I learned about God and tradition was, for the most part, in Sunday school and not in my home. For the most part, I embraced my Jewish identity as long as it would leave my dietary habits alone. Going to Hebrew school and the occasional Shabbat service was a chore I deeply resented because it bored me to pieces. Nonetheless, I figured it was my duty to my ancestors and the tiny Jewish community of my hometown to show up on a semi-regular basis.

The Judaism I grew up with was centered on community, social action, and a strong passion for Israel. While all those things are important, none of those values satisfied the desire I craved in my teen years, shortly after my bat mitzvah–a genuine relationship with God.

The name Jesus still has a funny taste in my mouth. To speak of him as a personal friend and not just a historical figure sometimes feels as obscure as attempting to explain my life story in Swahili.

While I can explain as well as I know my own address the reasons I am drawn to Christianity, there are some things I can never get used to, like admitting to others "I am a Christian" or "I have to go to church." "Christian-ese" is a language I hope to never become fluent in. To this day, I still can't stand common, clichéd expressions like "born again," "getting saved," "accepting Jesus into your heart," and my personal favorite: "quiet time with the Lord." Not having grown up in the church, I assumed these expressions were vocabulary used only by fundamentalists, and not "regular" church folk like my friends at school. That is one of many ways my Jewish upbringing makes me somewhat of an unusual Christian.

From learning new lingo to embracing different traditions, my Judaism continues to impact my

Christianity in both grand and miniscule ways. I've learned to get used to praying with my hands folded, but kneeling feels awkward because it reminds me how the Jews were once slaves to Pharaoh in Egypt, forced to bow only to him. But Jewish culture isn't without its own language and euphemisms too. "Oy vey!" is a phrase I will likely never outgrow. Social justice is an obligation of the Jews, so I used–and continue to use—the word *mitzvah* (meaning "act of kindness" in Hebrew) in my speech almost as often as the word "like" peppers the vocabulary of a Valley Girl. I still feel more inclined to use the word "mitzvah" in place of any English euphemism; it's simply stuck with me.

Part of me hopes I never get too comfortable "acting Christian." It would feel as if I'd lost whatever strands of Judaism I still have left to claim. My Jewish identity, I quickly discovered, is not something I can easily change like a pair of socks. My Jewish identity is as permanent to me as my skin, hair, and eye color, my right-handedness, and my blood type. I see the world through Jewish-colored lenses; I don't know how *not* to. I feel extreme compassion for minorities because I grew up as one. I am careful how I go about sharing my faith, because I understand the frustration of not having my beliefs taken seriously.

I think most Jews admire Jesus in a "look but don't touch" sort of way. I know I did. Throughout my life he was something of an enigma to me; someone I admired from afar like that popular high school boy I could never work up the guts to say hi to. From time to time I flirted with the idea of worshiping him, and feel a similar kind of rush as one felt by a teen girl who can't help dallying with that infamous bad boy her parents warned her to stay away from.

The more forbidden Jesus was to me, the more my curiosity about him grew. But because he was off limits to me, I also resented him for that wedge between Jews and Christians, which I assumed was his fault. I saw him as a political rebel whose only purpose was to cause trouble, not to bring redemption to a broken world. Still, there was a magnetic sort of attraction I attempted to resist every step of the way, bickering and picking fights with him as if we were already an old married couple.

No one will deny that Jesus was a great teacher

who said great things, but for the Jew, that's pretty much all that he is. The most popular question my Christian friends asked me growing up was why the Jews "rejected" Jesus as Lord and Savior, and there are many reasons for that.

First, I object to the use of the word "reject" in this context. You can deny or choose not to believe in the divinity of Christ, but to me you cannot "reject" someone who has never been a part of your life in the first place. The Jews "rejecting" Jesus as their savior is like a woman turning down a date from a man she has not yet met.

Jews do not believe that Jesus fulfilled all the Messianic prophecies, and the fact that Jesus claimed to be God in the flesh is enough to discredit his validity. This is because Judaism teaches that the Messiah, whoever he is, must be a man and *only* a man, nothing more. The Jewish Messiah is also expected to bring world peace in one visit; Jews do not believe he will need to make a second coming. There is also some debate about how Jesus, who is a descendant of King David, can claim messianic lineage because Joseph was not his earthly father. Ergo, because his biological parentage is through Mary alone, Jews do not believe he qualifies as the Messiah.

Jews are a lot like Catholics about harboring guilt. There have never been many Jews to begin with, but thanks to Hitler and the Holocaust, the number of Jews on earth has been reduced to less than 1 percent, and of that 1 percent, only a fraction consider themselves "practicing." To embrace Christianity, a religion with followers who actively persecuted Jews throughout history, is nothing less than betrayal. Lastly, since Christianity is the dominant religion of American society, and most Jews in America are decidedly liberal, Christianity is often associated with the raging fanatics who get their own pulpits on national television.

My family and remaining Jewish friends are becoming more accepting of my decision, but they may never understand it completely. To them, it probably seems as if I squandered my Jewish life the way the prodigal son squandered his father's money on frivolous, blasphemous things. But unlike the prodigal son, I have yet to return to the home of traditional Judaism. To them–and even to myself at times–I am always a prodigal daughter of sorts. I became lost, stranded far away from what is familiar. I still have yet to be "found."

It's as if I fled from one family–the Jewish community that raised me–and was subsequently adopted by a new family: the church. I have played the roles of both sons–the older one who followed the rules and did his share of the work out of legalistic duty, and the younger one who had to lose everything to learn how to truly live–yet, I still feel as if I have one foot permanently in both worlds. Regardless of how far a person can wander from home, she can never completely forget where she came from.

As a pilgrim on a quest to figure out who I am, I have to say that it is not my goal to prove to Jews why they need Jesus to be "complete." Such terminology reminds me of how small and patronized I felt when I'd run into (literally run into) evangelists on street corners who demanded to know if I was saved. It's easy to despise Christians for claiming to have a monopoly on the truth when the punishment for disagreeing is roasting at Satan's barbecue.

Jews and Christians have too much to learn from each other to remain at arm's length, afraid to cross invisible boundary lines. These two faiths, both profoundly different and profoundly similar, need each other.

I initially started writing this book as a way to explain my lengthy testimony to the curious Christians in my Bible study. It didn't start out as a book, however. I wanted a personal record for myself of how my faith came to be, but as I started writing, I realized my story began early in my childhood. Before long, the essay had taken a story-like form, and that's when I realized a full-blown book was necessary. But this book isn't just for my curious Christian friends; it's for the Jews as well–several of whom were personally affected by my conversion. I can't promise that my reasons will be satisfactory, but I felt I owed an explanation for my new prodigal life.

While the term "prodigal daughter" is not one I use proudly, it is nonetheless an accurate description of my journey. This is not a tale of being lost for a period of time and suddenly being found, nor is it a cautionary lecture to Jewish parents on what can happen if their children don't receive a quality Jewish education (though that is one way to interpret it). Instead, this is a story of the places I've been, the lessons I've learned, the doubts I still struggle with, and the pieces of wisdom I've picked up along the way.

1

My first run-in with Christianity happened when I was eight years old. My uncle had just passed away, and I had to miss a day of school for the funeral. My best friend at the time felt obligated to tell me that he was in hell because he didn't believe in Jesus.

As a Jew, and a young one at that, I had never heard of this place called hell before. My mother, furious, called that girl's mother, and I remember them talking on the phone for what seemed like hours. Not surprisingly, that was the end of our friendship.

Shortly after that, in a separate incident, a neighborhood girl was forbidden to play with me once her mother found out I was Jewish. She didn't want her daughter being exposed to "Christ-Killers." Once again, no one explained to me just what the big deal was, or how I could possibly be held responsible for the death of a man who existed roughly two thousand years before I was even *born*.

When it came to religion and politics in my family, the rule was "don't ask, don't tell." That much made sense. I learned very quickly after those incidents at eight years old that those topics had the power to ruin friendships and start wars. I followed that rule, but not too many of my friends did: a consequence of growing up in a small suburb, where everyone was white, Catholic, and very Republican. Anyone who was anyone attended Saint Catherine's, the largest Catholic Church around, and almost anything pertaining to the Jewish religion was lost on many of my classmates.

"You're *Jewish*?" I remember hearing on too many occasions to count. "What does that even *mean*?" The intellectual capacity of my elementary-aged self was advanced enough to explain that it meant I celebrated Hanukkah and not Christmas–nothing more. Naturally, I would be asked "So what is Hanukkah?" and that's when I got stuck. In my mind at the time, Judaism was lighting candles for eight nights in a row and getting eight nights of presents from my parents, not Santa Claus or any other mythical figure. I'd simply nod when classmates responded "So it's like the Jewish Christmas," for no other reason except to end the conversation already.

The no-Santa Claus issue was devastating to me at the time. I remember spending one Christmas Eve in my bedroom hoping and praying with all my little heart that Santa would make a mistake and bring presents to my house. That never happened, of course (I think I turned out okay in spite of it).

As every Jew knows, Christmas is for Chinese food and a movie, the only two places that stay open for the holiday. Since the Jewish population of my town was so small, my family and I would often be the only ones in the Chinese restaurant of our choice. Despite the complaints of loneliness I made every year on Christmas Day, those were the times I bonded most with my crazy family.

My parents both grew up in Long Island, but didn't meet until college. My mother can best be described as five feet, three inches of pure New York sass (with a Yale education): the exact stereotype of a Jewish mother if there ever was one (except she can't cook if her life depended on it). She was raised in a semi-conservative family. After enduring long, boring Passover Seders as a child, she swore that she would let her children decide for themselves how

Jewish they wanted to be.

My father, on the other hand, grew up in a more liberal home where only a Bar Mitzvah was a mandatory part of growing up Jewish. That was one thing my parents agreed on when it came to religious education for their children: Shabbat services and Hebrew school would be required up until the point of bar/bat Mitzvah. After that, my brother Greg and I were free to make our own religious choices. That meant it was up to us, and us alone, to decide whether to be Reform, Conservative, or Orthodox (or somewhere in between). I don't think my parents ever thought one child would someday make the choice to become a Christian.

The line between religious and cultural identity in Judaism is a blurred one. Judaism is unique in that one can be hereditarily Jewish without necessarily adhering to the letter of the law. Regardless of personal taste for ritual, every Jew was symbolically present when God gave the Ten Commandments to Moses on Mount Sinai. This, regardless of denomination, is what binds us all together.

That unshakable communal bond seemed more

user-friendly than the "Repent or burn" mantra of Christianity. That was far too exclusive for my taste, not to mention very unwelcoming. Whether they intended to do this or not (and I don't believe they did), I felt alienated by my non-Jewish friends. I envied the fact that there were enough of them to form a real community. Of all the families who regularly attended synagogue, only a fraction of them had children close to my age. Consequently, there were only seven people in my Bar/Bat Mitzvah class, and less than a dozen of my classmates were Jewish. If I wanted Jewish friends, I had to trek forty-five minutes to a city that my brother and I dubbed "Jewish" capital of Ohio because its synagogues rivaled Saint Catherine's in terms of size, community events for all ages, youth groups, and fun field trips.

I tried to initiate myself in the youth group meetings, the "retreats," and the services in Beachwood, but the kids I met there seemed as incredulous of the fact that I didn't attend BBYO, NFTY, USY or any of those well-known Jewish youth groups as my Catholic friends were of the fact that I didn't know what the Eucharist was. Those kids had the T-shirts, the wristbands, were hard-core fans of the Orthodox rapper Matisyahu, and attended all the right Jewish day schools. I simply did not fit in.

By the time I was about to enter middle school, my bat mitzvah was coming up and, quite frankly, I didn't understand the point. I slogged through Hebrew lessons and chanting my Torah portion over and over again for my Rabbi with nothing but impatience and contempt. Time and time again, I'd protest to Rabbi Friedman, "Who cares if it's not perfect?!" My Rabbi, who had been painstakingly correcting my pronunciation of the Hebrew for months on end, was unfazed. She was as dedicated to the thought of my being radically transformed by Torah as I was to passionately avoid it. "All my friends who are invited are Catholic," I protested. "They won't be able to tell if I make a mistake."

"Ahh," she replied, with the wisdom and patience that every great Rabbi must have, "but *you* will know. And so will *Adonai*."

All I could think was, *What I would give to just have a Communion service like everybody else*. But I managed to soldier on. After all, I reasoned, after the ceremony would be the biggest birthday bash I'd ever have.

While certainly not in my town, but definitely in other parts of the country, the lavish festivities of the Jewish Bar/Bat Mitzvah reception are rivals to those of MTV's *My Super-Sweet Sixteen*.

Little did I know what changes would take place after that. My childhood set the stage; it was after my Bat Mitzvah that the journey took off running.

2

There are certain dates that stand out as milestones in my mind–like the day a good friend of mine committed suicide, my first kiss, the day I got my driver's license, and the date of my high school graduation. The first of all these memorable days, however, is what happened on November 10, 2001, the day of my bat mitzvah.

Just days away from my thirteenth birthday, I was more concerned about my dress (a purple, flowery mini-gown that I fell in love with at first sight), my hair (curly and unmanageable, that day no exception), and my teeth (hurting from my new braces) than whether I'd remember the words of my Torah portion in front of the entire congregation. I was too out of touch to invite any boys from my class, so making *that* sort of impression wasn't an issue. When it came down to it, I wanted to look pretty and wow the pants off my gentile friends with my impressive Hebrew-chanting skills.

The irony of all this was that the ceremony was taking place in what used to be Saint Catherine's church before the parish upgraded to a larger building. Contrary to the stereotype, the lone Jews of my town did not have enough money to build a temple from scratch, so we were given permission to rent it out for a while as we saved up for a place of our own.

The old historic church was still adorned with crosses in the stained-glass windows. The basement walls were covered with crayon writings of "Jesus Loves Me," as it was still an active Christian day care center and preschool. The "Temple Beth Simcha" above the door made us look like Jews for Jesus. This, to me, is one of many proofs of God's sense of humor.

The service went smoothly, and my parents' Orthodox friends from New Jersey were impressed at the apparent harmony between Jews and Christians in this very strange town. While playing host to family members and posing for an endless amount of pictures was stressful, I could not deny a sense of peace and contentment up there on the *bimah*. How that happened or why was a mystery to me, since having a bat mitzvah at all wasn't a big deal to me at the time. That wasn't the moment my life changed forever, but that was the day my curiosity about God and religion suddenly came alive.

I can't say there was ever a time in my life when I was decidedly atheist. I suppose, like many people, I had a feeling there was *something* out there keeping the universe together, but whether that something was God was impossible to know. As melodramatic as it sounds, the first god I had in life was my hair. I didn't worship my unruly "Jew fro" by any means, but I made an idol of it in the sense that it controlled my moods more than is considered normal for a pre-teen girl. It would never be thin enough, shiny enough, or smooth enough for me to be happy and confident with my self-image.

It won't hold up in a court of law, but I know there *must* be a God because after my bat mitzvah, I started caring about religion at a time when many adolescents start to rebel against it. Despite twelve previous years of moaning and groaning about having to attend Shabbat services, I could feel my curiosity growing. That, to me, is nothing short of a miracle–especially because it wasn't too long before that I'd "dared" God by having the audacity to eat a slice of bacon on Yom Kippur, the Day of Atonement. If God existed, I reasoned, then surely he would strike me down for eating this slice of bacon, the most un-kosher food there is. But he didn't, so I decided I could eat whatever I wanted without the slightest twinge of guilt.

Amazingly, after my Bat Mitzvah I did start to feel twinges of guilt for not keeping kosher. This is not the most valid of excuses, but keeping kosher is just one of those things you have to grow up practicing, or else it's not going to work. Maybe it does for some people, but my family did not keep a kosher kitchen; kosher meat is more expensive than non-kosher meat, and my parents refused to splurge on an extra set of dishes and silverware. Naturally, the cafeteria at my school wasn't kosher either. Still, I'd find myself whispering apologies toward heaven every time I indulged in a cheeseburger. How nice it must be to be a Christian, I thought. *They* got to eat whatever they wanted–except for meat on Fridays during Lent, but that's much more doable than no mixing meat and dairy *ever*.

School pretty much remained the same, but eighth grade was probably the worst year of my grade school life. A few months in, I had a huge fight with my circle of friends (the cause of which was probably something ridiculous and mundane, but serious enough for middle school girls to end a friendship over) and I ate my lunch in the guidance office for a while. The death of a close friend of mine by suicide when I was fourteen (he was thirteen) was the next huge catalyst for pushing me toward God. It's one of those days that I remember with perfect clarity: what I wearing (navy sweatpants and a white T-shirt) and even the class I was sitting in when I heard other students whispering about it (Earth Science).

I had never been to a wake before (another thing Jews do not do, for which I am very grateful: open-casket funerals freak me out). I broke, not at the sight of Nathan's lifeless body (which, thanks to makeup, did not even look real), but at the tissue-paper butterfly placed in his hands. I don't know what it was intended to symbolize in that context–hope? healing?–but even as a fourteen-year-old girl, butterflies were more than just a cutesy trend; they were symbolic of a desire to live life to its fullest capacity. I could never view butterflies in the same way again.

Nathan's death catapulted my own bout with circumstantial depression, which only got worse when my dad was diagnosed with cancer.

With no close friends left to confide in, I felt completely and utterly alone. In my deep pit of despair, I bought a cheap notebook and began pouring my heart out to God in letters. It was the first time I felt any semblance of a relationship with him, and it meant more to me than hair, shopping, and boys–huge priorities in the life of a fourteen-year-old girl!

The God I wrote to in my journal, however, was a God I had fashioned in my head, and not the God of the Torah. The God I believed in imposed no rules, no judgment, and certainly no condemnation of sin (which was only for really, really bad people anyway). I owned a Bible with my full name inscribed on the cover–a gift from my Rabbi for my Bat Mitzvah–but it remained untouched and gathered dust on my bookshelf for quite some time. I heard some line of Christian-ese from my Catholic friends about how God wanted a "personal relationship" with us, and that's exactly what I was starting to create. Jesus was completely irrelevant to me. God and I were doing just fine without him.

I remember feeling absolutely *infuriated* by a flashing neon sign that a neighbor put up in his front yard every Christmas, claiming "Jesus is the reason for the season," complete with a nativity scene. Jesus constantly shifted between enemy and enigma. I had been told time and time again in Sunday school, at home, and by my Rabbi that it's okay to look at Jesus as a great teacher, but nothing more than that. Sometimes, I couldn't even give him that much credit.

Jesus, to me, was the reason for my loneliness. He stole my Catholic friends from me and ruined any chance of being fully included by them. I became increasingly paranoid around anyone who wore a crucifix around their neck, and since (unlike back in third grade) I was now old enough to understand what hell was, somehow I just *knew* that all Christians were out to convert me.

So it's interesting, then, why I had no problem participating in the community Christmas pageant for three years in a row. I suppose it had more to do with my desire to be seen onstage than to take part in a religious activity, but nonetheless I had my heart set on playing Mary (I was always cast as an angel in the chorus). That's how I learned all the religious Christmas songs that never make it on the radio. I found them beautiful; I'd just keep my mouth shut every time Jesus was mentioned.

Interestingly, my parents were supportive of this, but I wonder how it went explaining to my Sunday school teacher why I had to miss a few classes because I was needed at pageant rehearsals. It was during these pageant rehearsals that I met my friend Luke, who played a Wise Man, and would later enter the seminary for priesthood. He became the older brother I never had. It's also through him that I met my first gentile boyfriend, but that's another story.

My mixing with Christian friends and even dabbling in Christian rituals like pageants were fun and innocent as long as I understood where my boundaries were. It was frustrating having to always watch my guard, and it angered me that most of the kids in my bar/bat mitzvah class didn't seem to care as much about being Jewish as I did (or at least that's how I perceived the situation, since one's religious identity is very personal and complex).

Ironically, my desire to start going back to synagogue was still nonexistent. I wanted God, but not if I had to sit through boring sermons. Even if I'd wanted to go, it's not like I would have benefited much (this is what I told myself). The Rabbi gave thoughtful sermons about Jewish marriages, raising Jewish families, and living Jewish lives that were completely irrelevant to my budding adolescent self. My Christian friends, on the other hand, had their youth groups and their youth pastors to turn to for moral guidance, support, and age-appropriate life advice.

This wasn't an issue of Christianity being better than Judaism; there just wasn't enough Jewish youth to start a group like that in my town. My Rabbi did the best she could, but she was also a Rabbi for another congregation about an hour away, and her hands were always full.

I had to learn how to be Jewish on my own terms, and I quickly decided that rituals like keeping kosher, not spending money on Shabbat, and attending services every Friday evening were not for me. My determination and passion were fierce, to a point where, in seventh grade, I whipped out a highlighter and drew a sloppy Star of David on my forehead to shut up an obnoxious kid who made fun of me for not having an ash cross on my forehead like everyone else did on Ash Wednesday (after which he never dared to make fun of me again).

News of that incident traveled fast, and my reputation as "Super Jew" started to catch on. I can't say that I blame my Catholic friends for feeling slightly intimidated by me. Despite being just under five feet tall and roughly eighty pounds, I was very outspoken and made it quite clear to everyone that Jesus and I would never, ever get along–so don't bother trying to introduce us!

I dreaded the Mondays after every weekend retreat with Saint Catherine's youth group, because that was when practically every kid in school would show up in matching shirts with some ridiculous slogan on them. I'm not sure if it was a requirement to wear those shirts after every retreat, but it was extremely annoying to see every kid in school wearing one. For some odd reason, I found the slogans on these shirts amusing, even though many were in poor taste. Some of my favorites were "Stop Drop and Roll Doesn't Work in Hell" (the most offensive one I ever saw), and Jesus on a surfboard (yes, really) saying, "Hang ten with Jesus!" My creative form of protest was to wear my own "retreat" shirt to school on those Mondays. I got it from a Jewish volunteer program I participated in one summer. It had a plate-sized Star of David on the back.

One day I shocked the daylights out of my parents by telling them I had a desire to be confirmed (I was pretty shocked by it myself, actually). The tradition of Jewish confirmation is fairly new, established in more liberal denominations to cater to the epidemic of youth dropping out of Judaism following their bar/bat mitzvahs. It's basically a graduate-style ceremony that "welcomes back" older teens who wish to continue their Jewish education. It seemed very fitting for me, a growing teenager with an increasing appetite for God.

I'm still not sure whether it was a calling from God or a result of the non-Jewish environment I grew up in, but after my confirmation was complete, my mind was made up: I was going to become a Rabbi. I was fifteen years old.

3

My first boyfriend was a popular fifteen-year-old freshman named Ben, whom I was reluctant to go out with at first because I was a sixteen-year-old sophomore, and a year's difference between a guy and a girl at that stage of life meant a lifetime of difference in maturity. But because I had my heart set on being a Rabbi, I imposed a Jews-only rule when it came to dating. While his father was Catholic, he never went to synagogue, never had a bar mitzvah, and declared himself an atheist, Ben's *mother* was Jewish, and that was good enough for me (since Jewish heritage is traditionally passed on through the mother). In a school like mine where Jews were in the minority, I couldn't afford to be too choosy.

Our religious differences, among other things, were the biggest roadblock in our three-week long "relationship." He dumped me at lunchtime, and while I certainly wasn't head-over-heels in love with the guy, he *was* my first kiss, and I was devastated. So much, in fact, that I imposed on myself *another* rule: no dating in high school ever again. I'd just go to a Jewish college and find a nice Jewish boy there.

High school relationships were futile, anyway.

Naturally, shortly after I made that promise, another popular guy (a senior this time!) came along and swept me off my feet. I tried to be bold about my commitment to no dating, especially since this one was an Episcopalian. But emotions won out, and we got involved in an on-again, off-again pseudo-relationship that fizzled out within a year.

After much deliberation, I broke it off with him the summer before my senior year, which was when I met John at a graduation party. He was gorgeous, popular, *older*…and Catholic (with a closet full of those cheesy retreat shirts to boot). However, in spite of all that, by the end of that summer I was hopelessly, ridiculously, irrevocably, head-over-heels in love.

His parents didn't love me so much, though. It's just a theory, but I wonder if my goal of becoming a rabbi freaked them out a little bit (I was also a little young for him, which, in hindsight, should have been a warning). Some of my friends would later ask me if I became a Christian so his family would approve of our relationship, which hurt deeply. It made my quest for truth seem shallow and insincere. John would, in a very strange, twisted way, play a part in leading me to Christ, but I wouldn't realize it until several years later.

Long before the idea of becoming Christian concerned me, the issue of my hypocrisy in Judaism was becoming a real problem. It's one thing to agree and disagree with some Jewish concepts, but it's completely another issue to render them pointless because they did not pertain to my chosen lifestyle. As a wannabe rabbi, I couldn't keep myself from dating *goyim*–non-Jewish boys–much less uphold the laws of the Torah. How could anyone take me seriously? I couldn't even take myself seriously, and deep down I suspected God couldn't either.

To anyone who asked, I'd simply justify my pick-and-choose tendencies by insisting that I was going to be a *Reform* rabbi. If being female prevented me from being joining the clergy in Orthodox and Conservative temples, but I could get away with it in the Reform denomination, why couldn't I get away with my cafeteria style of Judaism, too?

Justifying my habits to myself only worked so far.

If I felt like a hypocrite in my own eyes, then clearly I had a problem. It was glaringly obvious that pleasing my congregation meant more to me than pleasing God. My heart was just not in it. According to Jewish tradition, going through the motions of ritual when the heart is full of doubt is eventually supposed to bring back the fervor and devotion, like pushing yourself to work out even if you don't always feel like it. The problem for me was the rituals I was expected to keep were ones I never had to begin with, so where did that leave me?

These feelings of inadequacy were reinforced during my first trip to Israel when I was seventeen. All my life, I'd heard Israel was a paradise, a place that every Jewish soul longs for, the one little corner of the world that is rightfully ours. I was thrilled to finally have an opportunity to go there for a volunteer program, and at the thought of being surrounded by hundreds of people just like me.

Unfortunately, I got a little too close to the Lebanese border at the wrong time, and was forced to evacuate when war broke out. My parents, terrified for my safety, refused to let me stay in the country any longer and bought me a ticket home. I was supposed to stay for six weeks, but only made it for two. Thankfully, one year later I got a second chance. My cousin was having her bat mitzvah in Jerusalem, and this time the entire family would be going.

The land itself certainly lived up to the hype. I was completely awestruck by the thought of walking on the same hallowed ground as the patriarchs I'd read about–not to mention the deserts were strikingly beautiful. It was so richly satisfying to feel the presence of God there. During my stay, I met an Orthodox girl around my age that voiced her disapproval when I talked about wanting to be a rabbi. For her, the disapproval was less about my being female and more about my choice of denomination. She said it didn't make any sense to "water down" Judaism; basically, I'm either Orthodox or nothing at all.

The way she and my extended family live is probably as close to the law as you can get. During Shabbat services, the men sat on one side of the congregation while the women sat in a corner behind a curtain. That made me angry. As far as observance of the Sabbath was concerned, the list of things they could not do was staggering: it is forbidden to flip light switches, flush toilets, shower, and much more. In the hotel where I stayed with my family, there was a special "Shabbat Elevator" that stopped on every floor so the Orthodox wouldn't have to press any buttons.

I could understand the significance of not shopping on the Sabbath, or turning off the TV, but such discipline that went as far as not flipping light switches seemed very legalistic to me. Would the Sabbath day be less meaningful if I drove to Starbucks to curl up on my favorite couch by the window and catch up on my prayer journal? I had so many questions, but for fear of sounding rude and judgmental, I kept them to myself.

At first glance inside the world of the Orthodox, I thought they were all certifiably nuts. The second emotion I felt, oddly enough, was jealousy. I did not possess nearly the same level of patience, devotion, and discipline to live that way. But not every Orthodox Jew lives by the law out of love for God. Like many American Christians, some Jews have no reason for their strict devotion other than obligations to their families and communities.

By the end of the trip, I ended up not feeling Jewish enough in a land that was supposed to feel like home. While I'm sure it wasn't my new Israeli friend's intent to make me feel bad about myself as a servant of God, I still returned to the States feeling extremely inadequate.

In Christianity, the point of the Old Testament commandments (otherwise known as the "Old Law") is to show that humans are incapable of keeping them–that our default "sinner state" will start to show the more times we fail. They say that God's purpose in establishing those laws was to highlight our desperate need for the redemptive work of Jesus on the cross.

This seemed to make sense in theory, but to believe it would require admitting to myself that I was imperfect; that I had flaws; that the presence of sin in my life was so offensive to God, he couldn't allow me into heaven without requiring me to give up and change everything about who I was.

I bristled at the insistence of Christians that the

God of the Old Testament was the same God as in the New Testament. The God of Judaism didn't require an innocent man to die for sins that weren't his fault. Furthermore, Jews are able to come to God directly rather than through a mediator. The Christian God seemed far too clique-ish for my liking. I was fine the way I was, thank-you-very-much.

Only I wasn't fine. I never managed to shake my feelings of hypocrisy every time I drove on the Sabbath or ate a bowl of ice cream just minutes after finishing a brisket dinner. I know many Reform Jews say it's liberating to pick and choose our rituals. That never worked for me; I felt like I was cheating. In hindsight, I felt I was doing Judaism a great disservice long before I welcomed Jesus into my life.

4

Most of the heroes I had growing up were Christian, from Elizabeth I to Cassie Bernall. The heroine who influenced me most was Joan of Arc–though admittedly, I might not have found her story as fascinating if not for her tragic martyrdom. I still have a collection of biographies about her today, but the first one I ever owned was for elementary-aged kids, told mostly through pictures. That should give you more of a clue of just how odd of a kid I was: other girls read the Babysitter's Club, and I was reading up on a saint who was burned to death. Normal stuff.

Martyrdom has always intrigued me: Is the person who chooses an agonizing death rather than renouncing their beliefs just crazy, when it would be easier to deny them and live? If I were threatened with being tied to a stake and burned alive, what would I do?

I believed in the slogan WWJD-What Would Joan Do? Perhaps being female and closer to my age made her a more relatable role model. Or maybe it was the idea that one need not be rich, educated, or exceptionally beautiful in order to change the world. Joan of Arc was none of those things, and she didn't need to be. She only had to believe in the importance of her mission. At one point in my young life, I had a dream about her and woke up convinced it was a sign that I *was* her, reincarnated (just don't ask me to explain how a medieval Catholic saint gets reincarnated in the body of twentieth-century Jewish girl, because logic had no part in that fantasy).

My fascination with Saint Joan probably leaned more toward unhealthy obsession by the time I entered middle school. It was because of her–rather, her legend–that virginity and physical purity became something of an idol to me: a measurement of my worth as a servant of God. I was not mature enough to understand how fear of sexuality was woven into the fabric of medieval life–so much that virginity (particularly for women) was venerated to an almost magical status.

The rules I set in place to guard my purity were almost identical to those of most evangelical church groups: I drew the line at hand-holding and chaste kisses, and harshly judged my classmates who went beyond that. Forget keeping kosher and the Sabbath, and all those other "rules": so long as I safeguarded my virginity until marriage, I was being faithful to God and would have no problem being welcomed into heaven (it's interesting that I had a somewhat solidified idea of the afterlife, when Judaism is pretty silent on the issue. I believed heaven was real, and hell was for Hitler).

By the time I was seventeen years old, a senior in high school on the cusp of graduation, I was one hundred percent certain of God's will for my life. My purpose was to change the world through Judaism: to become a rabbi and create a synagogue that not only had sermons relevant for people of all ages, but also included youth group activities (with T-shirts!) so every Jewish teen would have a place to belong. Maybe, with a little luck, I could even become the first Jewish saint.

Yes, I was that self-righteous.

On the "Ambitions" page of my senior yearbook, the graduating class of 2007 listed their goals and future plans. Some wrote about wanting to get married, have babies, and make lots of money. My entry was this solitary sentence: "I want to change the world by becoming a rabbi." I had forgotten that was in there until one day I felt nostalgic and pulled it off the closet shelf to reminisce. Reading those words again brought tears to my eyes. Part of me thought *how foolish to think I knew everything when I was barely old enough to vote*. The other part of me longs to remember what that kind of certainty feels like. How I wish I could be as certain about who I am now as I was back then.

The good news is, I'm not seventeen anymore. I'm now aware how few people stick to the same career plans that were made before being old enough to drive a car. Many people in their thirties and beyond are still unsure about the life they are "supposed" to have. That's an oddly comforting thought.

Sometimes it feels clear that God used certain life events like puzzle pieces, slowly forming a complete picture. I think foreshadowing is a literary technique that God is quite fond of in the bible, as indicated by the many prophecies of the Old Testament. Not every biblical character lived to see the outcome of his or her faith. Abraham was long dead by the time his descendants became "as numerous as the stars." Ruth had no idea that converting to Judaism would earn her a place in the lineage of Jesus.

I don't know how much I believe the expression "everything happens for a reason." But I do believe God can redeem broken things that feel hurtful or senseless. That's the underlying message of the gospel. I would love to see the following message on a bumper sticker someday: *Shit happens, but shit makes good fertilizer.*

I think about the Nature versus Nurture debate more than is probably normal. Had I grown up in a more Jewish-populated area, had I been given the finest Jewish education that Ohio has to offer, and had books about medieval saints been completely off-limits, would I still have felt drawn to Jesus? If a psychologist examined my life under a microscope, it might seem obvious that my Jewishness fell apart due to a lack of Jewish education and influence. To what extent does a person become a product of his or her environment?

I had the right kind of passion and zeal for rabbi-hood; I just didn't have the right kind of focus. I was driven by a need for community, not a desire to teach the Torah: something I would have realized if I ever made it to Jewish seminary.

Some Christian friends have told me they envy me for being a "Jewish Christian" (not a phrase I use to describe myself) because I got the privilege of growing up with the same rituals Jesus himself practiced. Still, there is always a feeling of apprehensiveness in my gut because of what I had to give up. As much as I try to convince myself that I am gaining more than I am losing, the reality is that I gave up quite a lot. By embracing Jesus I have severed all spiritual ties with the Jewish community. No more invitations to Seders and Hanukkah parties. No more reciting the *shema* prayer without people thinking I'm speaking in tongues.

Do I believe that the Old Testament prophecies point directly to Jesus? I don't have a degree in biblical history or fluency in ancient Hebrew; I can't say for sure. What I tell people is this: I became a Christian because this man called Christ seems worth knowing. A man who showed compassion to prostitutes and lepers, soiling his chance to be one of the 'in' crowd of Pharisees, and was willing to die for his enemies, is someone worth living for.

But following Jesus always comes with a cost, and for me that cost is giving up my right to call myself a Jew. I've met Christians who insist I can have it both ways–I can call myself a Christian by faith, a Jew by heritage–but to insist I'm still Jewish feels intellectually dishonest.

I liked that Christianity seemed to have its mind made up about its beliefs. Judaism's answers to life's most important questions vary depending on which denomination you choose. I always wondered: Was God just being metaphorical when he gave the laws to Moses, or not? Who are we to determine which traditions are worth keeping, and which are not?

Keeping kosher, a basic staple of the Orthodox life, was my biggest stumbling block: no matter how much I read up on the subject to try and understand it better, I simply couldn't wrap my mind around why God cared what we ate when the world is full of suffering and evil.

Simply put, keeping kosher isn't something that brings me closer to God. I was attempting to do it for brownie points, not because it meant something personal to me. Then again, sometimes prayer feels like an exercise in nothingness. The words that roll off my tongue may be holy, but sometimes I'll be simultaneously thinking about my weekend plans or what I'll wear to work the next day. With keeping kosher, I might be able to pat myself on the back for doing well to keep the law, but if my heart is grumbling about the pointlessness of it, then why bother? I know God cannot be fooled.

I know now that God is bigger than petty things like emotions. I forced myself to admit that I didn't keep kosher because I just didn't want to, even though God apparently thought it was important. The Jewish guilt continued.

But dietary restrictions aside, there were other unresolved issues. Every Christian I knew was taught to pray in English, not Hebrew, and talk to God like he was a close friend. In Judaism, there are prayers for just about every occasion, including a prayer of thanks for bowel movements. To my knowledge there is no "official" Hebrew prayer to cope with the devastation of breaking up with a boyfriend, the stress of going off to college, or the peace of mind to deal with annoying co-workers. Praying in Hebrew is beautiful, but not always convenient for every situation. Not for me, anyway.

The first time I went to Israel with my family, a friend of my mom's asked her to pray for her sick husband at the Western Wall, to which my mom responded, "Sure, I'll pray for him Caplin-style." When she told me about this I asked, "What do you mean, 'Caplin-style'?" She replied, "It means I'll go to the wall and recite the prayer over the Shabbat candles, because that's the only prayer I know." Neither of us had been taught to pray as if God was sitting across from us with hot cocoa and a compassionate shoulder to cry on.

Somehow I knew God loved me, but my inability to maintain the laws of Torah was starting to reveal the existence of a stubborn, sinful nature. Gone were the days of worshiping the God I imagined in my head who imposed no rules, because that was breaking another law: the one against idolatry.

5

I wasn't sure what to make of Anne the first time I met her. We had a mutual friend, Luke, in common, who introduced us. Like me, her unusual calling made her something of an oddball in high school: she wanted to join a convent after college. I now had two friends pursuing life in the clergy, thus making us the proverbial Priest, Nun, and Rabbi who went into a bar. In fact we did all go to a bar once, just so we could say we did it.

Unlike Luke, who understood my convictions were not to be questioned, thus limiting any talk of religion, Anne was fascinated by me. She dubbed me her "favorite little Jew" (let alone I was the only Jew she knew) and religion eventually became the sole focus of our conversations. I didn't mind talking about it with her, though. Something just glowed about her, and she quickly became one of my closest friends. I would always say that if I ever became a Christian, I'd want to be one like her.

She was the one person I trusted enough to ask all my questions about Christianity–the ones I kept to myself because I didn't want to risk having a sermon launched at me. It was Anne who, for the first time ever, explained the gospel in a way that made more sense than I thought it would: God's plan of redemption for a world marred by sin. Jesus was the final sacrifice for our sins. *Okay*, I thought. *I guess that's noble and everything.* But I still had trouble believing Jesus was the *only* way to God (most days I still do).

Much to my relief, Anne explained that the Jews could not be solely blamed for killing Jesus; we all killed him with our sin. My contempt for Christianity lessened, but not completely. It would take a few more years for that to happen. At the very least, she catapulted my curiosity even more. I kept pounding her with my questions, and she didn't mind at all.

By then, high school was almost over. My dream of attending a Jewish college so I could meet my Jewish husband wasn't going to come true. I ended up choosing Kent State because I got a free ride, thanks to my mom's position as a professor of nursing. *No worries*, I thought. I'd meet my Jewish husband at Hebrew Union College, where I'd eventually go for seminary training (God help our poor future children, with two rabbis for parents!).

I majored in English Literature and minored in Jewish Studies. The Hillel Jewish Student Center was just off campus: a former frat house with floors that creaked and no heat, making winter services freezing. But the faces were friendly and the atmosphere was mostly liberal, so it was a perfect home away from home. Not to mention the matzo ball soup, made from scratch every Friday, was delicious.

I quickly found out, however, that most students there were not as religious as I was–or as I was attempting to be, I suppose is more accurate. I was hoping to meet more future rabbis, but I was the only one. People there acted just as surprised to find that out about me as my gentile friends back home. I was slightly disappointed, but still attended every service and every event religiously (bad pun intended).

In addition, I helped out with advertising and publicity. Looking back today, it's clear that my attempts to spread the word about Hillel were quite evangelistic. I never would have used *that word* back then, but subconsciously I knew I was being a tad vindictive. It's as if I was trying to get back at all the people who'd tried to convert me by telling anyone and everyone how great *my* place of worship was. For anyone who wasn't sold by the idea of attending a service in a language they didn't understand, I'd try roping them in by bragging about how orgasmic the matzo balls were: way better than anything served in the campus dining halls.

Before long, a boy with not one, but *two* Jewish parents (hallelujah!) caught my eye, and apparently I caught his too. A mutual friend told me he was asking about me. When I admitted that yes, I did find him attractive, she made it her duty to play matchmaker. By the end of the week I had myself a date, even if all we could afford was dinner on campus.

We talked for hours, and everything was going smoothly until we stumbled across the subject of career plans. He wanted to be a marine biologist. When I told him I wanted to be a rabbi, his jaw dropped as if I'd insulted his mother. Suddenly we had nothing more to talk about. He walked me back to my dorm, where he said–I kid you not–"I really like you, but I don't see this going anywhere. *You're too Jewish for me."*

At first I thought he was kidding, or that I imagined it. Did another Jew seriously just tell me I'm "too Jewish"? Was there such a thing? My extended family in Israel could be considered "too Jewish." Didn't he know I ate bacon and drove my car on the Sabbath? The nerve of him!

Needless to say, that was the end of our brief courtship. I was angry for some time, perhaps to the point of absurdity. He was insane, clearly. Surely it had nothing to do with *me*. The girl who set us up was just as crushed as I was, and went back to her day job, since clearly her match-making skills weren't that sharp. That was as close as I ever came to dating another Jew.

College has a way of forcing you to be more open-minded. I was more than tolerant of differing religious viewpoints, but I still had yet to shed my irrational fear that all Christians were out to get me. This paranoia was again validated when I left my dorm for class one day and was approached by a girl who introduced herself as Stephanie. She had a cheerful, friendly voice that suddenly felt less cheerful and friendly when she handed me a flyer for Campus Crusade for Christ. Cru, as it is commonly called, seemed like every Christian youth group I'd ever heard of, complete with matching T-shirt logos (seriously, what is the deal with Christian groups and their matching T-shirts?). She asked me to fill out my contact information on a little "get to know you" card. Not wanting to be rude, I took two minutes of my time to fill it out, and then went along my merry way.

By the end of the week, Stephanie had emailed me to ask about having lunch together sometime. Nothing was said about Jesus or Cru's weekly meetings, but I was smart enough to read between the lines and understand her true motives. I'll admit, my response was not very classy or tactful: "I know what you're trying to do," I wrote, "and you need to know that I'm happy being Jewish. I want nothing to do with Jesus, so if that's what this is about, don't bother writing back."

There may have been a few swear words in there too. I don't quite remember.

At the time, I was defending my faith and standing up for every Jew who had been the victim of street-corner evangelism. I considered myself a crusader of sorts, but not of the "for Christ" variety. Cru's mission statement, as written on their website, was to transform the campus for Christ, and mine was to transform it for Judaism. I clicked the "send" button and imagined I was a soldier engaged in spiritual mortal combat: a Jewish Joan of Arc, saving the world from closed-minded evangelists. Let the games begin!

6

While I considered myself a nonconformist in my own right, I still tried to "Christianize" my Jewish faith in the subtlest of ways. Christianity is, after all, the dominating religion in America, and its influence seeps everywhere from the Pledge of Allegiance to business policies (what Starbucks has reduced hours for the observance of Hanukkah or Ramadan?). I guess it's possible I did many "Christian" things without really seeing them as explicitly Christian.

For instance, I wasn't aware it was a strict Christian-only policy to pray with one's hands folded. I just thought that was how prayer worked in general, so when I was caught praying in Temple with my hands clasped piously, mom quickly put them in my lap and said "Jews don't do that." Kneeling while praying is also off limits, because the Jews were forced to kneel before Pharaoh when they were slaves in Egypt–something I also didn't know until I tried it in synagogue and was promptly scolded for it. Oops.

To pray as a Jew, I could either sit or stand, with

my hands covering my eyes or simply hanging at my sides. But that all seemed like a battle over trivialities: why did it matter what position one prayed in, so long as one bothered to pray at all?

Christian cultural influence also affected the way I talked to God. Addressing him as "Father" felt more personal than traditional Hebrew titles, *Adonai* (lord, ruler) or *Hashem* ("the name"). You could say I was already living a double life: there was the side of me who wanted to stay organically Jewish, both out of hereditary duty and defiance to cultural norms, and then there was the part of me that was desperate to assimilate–if only to prove to my gentile friends I was just as capable of having a relationship with God as they were.

Still, the effects of living in a Christianized culture never ceased to annoy me. You never hear about "the Jewish thing to do" or even "the human thing to do" regarding acts of kindness. No, you only hear about "the Christian thing to do," because only Christians are capable of compassion, apparently. It also angered me a lot more than it should have when people wished me a Merry Christmas, not Happy Holidays;

automatically assuming I was "one of them," just an ordinary gentile. As envious as I was of other Christians, the "normal" ones, I also sincerely believed the world would be a better place if Christianity did not exist.

So it's a tad ironic, the way I drew closer to my Catholic (*very* Catholic) friend Anne. Maybe the Holy Spirit lurking within her worked like a magnet on my ever-growing spiritual curiosity. After my freshman year of college, her junior year, she dropped out to finish her education at a convent in Maryland. She literally gave away all her possessions, from her iPod down to most of her wardrobe. The order she chose was strict, and virtually no communication with the outside world was allowed. She shut down her Facebook account and her email. The only way to reach her was through good old-fashioned letter writing.

I was invited to attend Anne's final mass at Saint Catherine's, where the entire congregation would host a send-off party and extend their blessings for her journey into convent life. I sat with Luke and his family, and remained seated as everyone stood up to receive the Eucharist. I could feel some stares, which was awkward, but I endured it for Anne's sake.

After mass, Luke made it his duty to introduce me to everyone as "the future rabbi." He also added, "This is her first mass!"

I resisted the urge to throttle him. I was there for Anne and didn't feel like calling unnecessary attention to myself, the lone Jew who saw Jesus as nothing more than a wise prophet. I felt very disrespectful.

I didn't know how to explain this to my priestly friend, though. "What, are you embarrassed or something?" he asked.

"No," I stumbled. "I just don't think now is the right time or place—"

We were interrupted by Father William, who must have overheard our conversation because he looked at me with sudden interest and said, "A rabbi, huh?"

Luke slung his arm around me and beamed, as if he'd come up with the idea all on his own. "That's right!"

"Interesting." I felt uncomfortably aware of the

weight of my Star of David pendant hanging from its silver chain around my neck. Luke went on to mingle with other people, and I really wanted to find Anne, but I couldn't be rude to her priest (that would be a major sin, wouldn't it?).

I prepared myself to be tolerant during a series of "duh" questions about rabbis and Judaism as a whole, which I know was very judgmental of me. I stood corrected when instead we ended up having a fairly deep discussion about what it's like to be called by God, and how to know where he wants to lead us.

"It's so wonderful when young people feel called to commit their lives to the Lord," Father William said. He described the process of realizing he was called to be a priest, which led me to ask him, literally out of the blue, "Was there ever a 'defining moment' you had, when everything made perfect sense and you suddenly realized exactly what God wanted you to do with your life?"

Being a priest, I figured this would be an easy question. My spirits sank a bit when his face revealed confusion, not certainty.

"Well," he answered, slowly, "I don't believe in 'defining moments,' honestly. Convictions are a process. Sometimes they're only realized after a series of wrong turns. But when God is nudging you to do something, I think you'll definitely know it. It's impossible to ignore something like that."

At the time, I interpreted his words to mean that maybe God wasn't calling me to be a rabbi after all. Maybe that was something only *I* wanted. Maybe, instead, I was being called to write Jewish books, become a Sunday school teacher, or something not related to Judaism at all. I had no way of knowing that, within one year's time, I'd chuck rabbi-hood altogether and be worshiping Jesus.

I expected to say formal goodbyes to her at the mass, but it turned out Anne was able to arrange a last-minute lunch date just two days before her departure. There was something very somber about her, yet peaceful. It was mind numbing for me to see how willingly she gave up everything familiar and comfortable to follow God where she believed he wanted her to go–a process known to Christians as "picking up your cross."

Me, I couldn't even give up cheeseburgers or non-Jewish boys. This girl gave up all modern forms of technology, nice clothes, and was resigning herself to a life without *sex*. So either she was absolutely crazy, or all this Jesus stuff she kept telling me about was the real deal.

Well, I'm no psychiatrist, but Anne seemed way too grounded and balanced to me to be considered crazy. Televangelists and the Westboro Baptist Church of Kansas–the one that pickets military funerals with the "God Hates Fags" signs–were crazy, but Anne's devotion was in a league completely of its own. It was unlike anything I'd ever known or seen…and I wanted it. Badly.

I believe right there in Panera Bread, where I admitted I was jealous of Anne's faith, was when my life began to shift. I was the Titanic, hurtling faster toward the iceberg despite my best attempts to steer clear. All I could do was hold my breath and tense up, waiting for the inevitable. That "iceberg" called Christianity really seemed like a certain death: the death of my Judaism, and maybe even the end of several relationships. Some of my Jewish friends at

Hillel might dump me. What if my own family disowned me?

Once I stepped out of Panera and officially parted ways with Anne, I got in my car and slapped myself back into reality. "Wake up," I told myself. "You're a Jew. You have your place. Remember that."

That became my new mantra: *You're a Jew, you're a Jew, you're a Jew.* But my heart was slowly tearing at the seams; I caught myself playing that risky "What If" game. "What if" I became a Christian? Would I even be a good one? How much different would my life be? Would everything suddenly come together? Would all the questions I've ever had about life, death, and faith be answered?

While I longed for absolution in the deepest depths of my soul, in reality I knew that all I would end up with, should I dare to embrace this Jesus figure, would be an identity crisis.

If religion is like marriage, I was probably too quick to call a lawyer and arrange for a divorce. I should have done the responsible thing and sought every counseling method available to save my relationship with Judaism *before* allowing my eyes wander in the direction of a forbidden carpenter–that crazy man who claimed "I am the way, the truth, and the life." Judaism wasn't working for me; it was leaving me restless and unfulfilled, so *of course* I was liable to fall for such a ridiculous line as that one.

But this was more than just a forbidden attraction: it was warfare. There were strong, spiritual forces involved that began duking it out, fighting over who would eventually claim my heart.

They believed different things, these suitors: one believed in an afterlife, the other was undecided. One believed in Original Sin; the other believed we were all okay as long as we treated each other with respect. One said it was forbidden to eat pork; the other claimed Jesus eradicated the need to follow Old Testament laws.

Many could play, only one could win.

7

New experiences have always scared me. I don't deal with conflict very well; it's my tendency to run from it rather than deal with it directly. My default personality can be rude, selfish, and stubborn. I hate losing arguments and having to say I'm sorry.

But despite all that, I can see that I am becoming a new creation. The problem is, because I am being transformed through Jesus, the new creation I am becoming is heretical as it is beautiful.

By the end of my first college semester, my father, who had battled cancer on and off ever since I was in middle school, was diagnosed again. The disease was more aggressive this time. They say that there are no atheists in foxholes, and it seemed my entire world had sunk into quite a deep one this time.

In the middle of all this, my on-again, off-again relationship with John (if you could even call it that) was becoming increasingly complicated. At this point I uncomfortably accepted a "carpe diem" type philosophy about dating. If a guy liked me–and honestly, not many did (never the ones I *wanted* to like me)–I dated him. Or made out with him (in college it's hard to tell the difference sometimes). With John, that line was so blurred I had no idea what was happening, yet for some odd reason I believed I was still in love.

Middle school was when the Catholic youth group teens signed True Love Waits pledges. Synagogues don't really do that, but I thought it was cool (you understand by now I was a very strange kid, right?) so I wrote my own purity pledge in my journal. No one taught me that God intended for sex to be saved exclusively for marriage, but I knew it was what he wanted for me (no small thanks to my obsession with Joan of Arc). Funny thing is, when you're a nineteen-year-old virgin and convinced you've met the love of your life, it becomes easier to make exceptions to the so-called purity rules.

Especially when the pressure put on you by said love of your life continues to get worse, and you begin to feel you have less choice in the matter. I remember very clearly the first time I ever said "No" to John, and tried to move his hands away. He just smirked and said, "What do you expect? You're too hot for me to keep my hands off you." An odd thing to say when I was wearing sweatpants–not exactly my first choice of "asking for it" clothes.

Worship, I learned, is more than just bowing down and praising something; it's whatever or whomever your life revolves around. I was convinced my life would be empty without John. *John* convinced me my life would be nothing without John. Eventually, my convictions started to unravel because I was terrified of losing him…but I ended up losing myself in him instead. I was in way over my head before I could recognize the name of the kind of relationship I was experiencing: abusive. I didn't think that was possible in so-called loving relationships, and John was a good Catholic. He still regularly attended Mass, and everyone who knew him there loved him. He would never deliberately hurt me.

I had well-intentioned friends, including Anne, who tried staging an intervention about how unhealthy our relationship was becoming, but I refused to listen. Nothing seemed to make sense anymore. I was nowhere near ready to accept the severity of what was happening.

My quest for spiritual truth was still very important to me, even if my priorities were a mess. It was time to start taking matters into my own hands. I continued attending Shabbat services at Hillel, while at the same time soaking up as much comparative religious material as I could get my hands on. I pored over C.S. Lewis and sat riveted through memoirs by Anne Lamott and Lauren Winner. I also read Harold Kushner and Adin Steinsaltz. Hell, I even reread the *Diary of Anne Frank*.

The literature was helpful and encouraging, but not quite satisfying. Here's the bottom line: no perfect ending exists when you move from one faith to another. There is always going to be some lingering of what is familiar, some reminder of what it is that you have lost. Religion can be a lot like a tattoo: it has a way of digging deep beneath the skin, and thus can never be completely scratched out.

I could identify with the words of liberal and conservative Jews alike in the books I read, but the whole pick-and-choose aspect was still there. It was as if *how* you were Jewish didn't matter, just as long as you *were* Jewish, and there was no right or wrong way to go about it (except believing in Jesus, the false Messiah, of course).

To be Jewish is like being American, in a way: If you're born here, you're automatically a citizen. You can move away to Germany, Switzerland, or Afghanistan and still retain an American identity. Unless you decide to become a terrorist. Then you get arrested for treason. If you're a Jewish-born Christian you forfeit your Judaism, and the ancient rabbis would have had license to execute you for heresy (as many of the Jewish-born disciples were).

Then there's Christianity: a religion no one is born into, but something that you choose–a religion where salvation is determined by deliberately placing your faith in Jesus, and has nothing to do with how you were raised or what your parents believe. It's easy for a Jew to be a Jew because of his family's background, but scripture clearly states that following Christ must be an informed choice: a decision that is made daily.

Despite my turmoil, I kept my quest for faith a secret as best I could. I couldn't talk to Jews or Christians about it since both parties were biased. Even my atheist friends were no help; most of them grew up in Christian homes (which, as one snidely remarked, is *why* he is an atheist today. I wouldn't know).

I was able to talk to one friend, a girl I knew from high school who believed that some higher being existed: a Zeus-like figure whose sole responsibility was to dole out karma. She basically instructed me to do whatever made me happy, as long as I don't hurt anybody.

Well, that advice had just one teensy little bug in it–to do "whatever makes me happy" would require devastating a great number of people.

First and foremost, my mother.

8

I put off telling my mother–or anybody else, for that matter–about my "spiritual crisis" because I didn't need anyone else's opinion muddying my own. I was confused enough already.

I became obsessed with absolutes and, thanks to my obsessive-compulsive disorder, needed to have all the answers boxed neatly in perfectly organized rows. I had so much chaos bouncing in my head; my attempts to pray through it were futile with new "What if?" fears. "What if" I was disowned? How would I provide for myself? Where would I live?

Deep down I knew my family would never do that. But fear is powerful: it can make you believe anything.

It may seem dramatic, but this quest for spiritual truth was taking over my life so seriously that my eating habits changed, I wasn't sleeping very well, and I couldn't make myself relax. My grades didn't falter, though much of my attention span did. I was terrified at the thought of dying without having all the answers, and what my punishment would be if I chose the wrong path. What if I spent the rest of my life confused? Would I always be concerned what my family and friends thought of me? Would I let that fear dictate who I chose to become?

I tell people now that I lived in a closet: a spiritual closet, to be exact. I can't help wondering if closeted homosexuals feel a similar way.

When my dad woke up from his last surgery, I visited him in the hospital and asked if he'd seen any of the proverbial white lights while under heavy anesthetics, like in the movies. He said no; it was all just a blank darkness, with no indication of how much time had passed. It felt like he blinked when the IV was inserted and next thing he knew, he was awake in the recovery room.

His response disappointed me, but it's more than likely such visions are just wishful science fiction.

I also asked him if he ever felt the urge to pray before a surgery. He admitted to re-examining his beliefs about God, but it was nothing like an episode of *Touched by an Angel*. Even without any deep religious convictions, he faced his disease with bravery.

One afternoon while driving to the mall with my mother, I decided to spill the beans. I wasn't going to tell her I was changing religions all of a sudden, but I finally felt brave enough to casually mention some of the doubts I'd been having. I figured that it couldn't hurt to tell her then, when we were both in a good mood, as opposed to right after she reminded me for the eleventh time to unload the dishwasher.

It was a really dumb decision. Her face tightened and somehow she was able to figure out, without my explicitly mentioning so, that Christianity was what I was starting to look into (psychic mom-powers, I tell you).

She asked me not to tell any other family members just yet; a revelation like this had to be dealt with using extreme caution. All I could do was nod. I wanted to protest, but I just couldn't do it. I stared out the window, having completely lost all my desire to shop (and for me to not feel like shopping meant something serious).

Now I was more terrified than ever before that my fate as a spiritual orphan had officially been sealed. How I wished that I could call up Anne and tell her what had happened. She would understand and have some comforting words to say. She told me her story about converting to Catholicism when the rest of her family was Protestant. At the time I couldn't understand why it was such a big deal; all the denominations of Christianity sort of blurred together in my mind. They all worshiped Jesus, right? So what was the problem?

That was before I heard about Martin Luther and the whole Reformation business. Anne *did* face scorn from a few family members. However, she understood this was just the price of following God with her whole heart. My life felt empty without her there, now that I could finally relate.

After that day, Mom acted like that conversation in the car had never happened. In some ways I was grateful, but it frustrated me because it was unfinished. I was terrified to bring up the subject again, but I still wished there was some way I could make her understand just how difficult it was for me, that I couldn't just shed everything that made me Jewish like dandruff in dry weather.

To make matters worse, dinnertime discussions

started to get heated. My family has always been unusual in that we never really talked about how our days went or what we kids did in school. We talked politics and current events instead.

One night my brother mentioned a girl in his class who updated her Facebook status to say how excited she was to celebrate Christmas and Hanukkah, because she has one Christian and one Jewish parent. My then seventeen-year-old brother thought such a concept was ridiculous. Like me, he'd lost all interest in services after his Bar Mitzvah and had no desire to keep kosher. He did, however, participate in a youth group centered on Israeli advocacy and briefly considered joining the Israel Defense Force after college.

Not surprisingly, I lost my appetite and excused myself to my room, where I cried harder than I had in a long time. The last time I'd cried that hard was probably when my friend Nathan killed himself back in eighth grade.

For the first time, the thought of losing my family's respect felt *real*. So what exactly was it about this Jesus that was becoming more and more attractive to me? What was it about him that was worth the risk of losing some, if not all, of my family and friends?

The idea of a god in the flesh is probably the most serious form of blasphemy a Jew could ever commit. I, however, loved the imagery of a god who understood perfectly the way it felt to cry with your whole body, to feel loneliness as agonizing as a salted scalpel. Most of all, God in the form of Jesus knew all too well how it felt to be betrayed by the ones you thought you could trust the most.

This conviction that Jesus might really be God sank in my stomach like a swallowed brick. It hurt in the best possible way: but how could something so terrifying motivate me to be brave?

9

Over the years I've collected many different bibles. The first one I ever owned was a gift for my bat mitzvah, with my full name embossed on the cover in gold. It was too fancy for practical use, so I bought my first "study bible" at a Jewish bookstore. Within a few months I had marked up and dog-eared it to the point where it was starting to fall apart, so I patched it up with duct tape and colorful stickers.

My dad gave me the bible he'd received for his bar mitzvah as a confirmation present, and that bible sat on my dresser opened to Proverbs 3:5-6, which says "Trust in the Lord with all your heart, and commit all of your ways to him. Lean not on your own understanding, and he will make your paths straight." I had to get a Hebrew-English bible for my college Hebrew class (then a prerequisite for my training as a rabbi), and a staff member from Hillel, who took a special liking to me my freshman year, gave me a pocket-sized book of Psalms.

I got my first copy of the New Testament completely by chance. Years ago, I was at my friend

Gina's house while she was cleaning out her closet, and she recovered a dusty copy of a bible, complete with the New Testament: a gift from her grandmother one Christmas. An outspoken atheist, Gina was going to throw it away. Before I could think twice about it, I asked if she'd let me have it instead. A book was a book regardless of subject matter; throwing it away would just be a waste of paper. I figured I'd donate it to the local library.

Instead, it ended up residing in *my* closet, completely untouched until one day *I* decided it was time to get rid of all the junk lurking in there. I held it carefully and outstretched the way one might hold a stingray. It just felt so scandalous; I was half afraid that the imaginary Heretic Police would arrive and confiscate it. But curiosity got the better of me, and before I knew it, I'd spent the next hour flipping through the Gospels. Reading about the life of Jesus was interesting, but the book I came across that resonated the most was Romans–particularly chapter seven, where the Apostle Paul talks about longing to do what is right, but giving in to what he knows is wrong instead. It seemed like an odd inclusion, for a book that was supposedly a litany of dos and don'ts.

If human beings could redeem and justify themselves, Christians teach, there would have been no point to Jesus dying on the cross. Even though I still had more searching to do, I was already convinced that *if* I became a Christian, I wouldn't be the wishy-washy, lukewarm type that demanded free grace without the cost of the cross. My sin, whether I liked it or not, even though I didn't feel like "that bad" of a person, had serious consequences.

I wasn't "technically" Christian yet, but still I felt a need to start cleaning up my life. I didn't break up with John per se, but I did tell him I was done fooling around. He didn't take that news very well. When he tried telling me how much he loved me and how much I meant to him, I finally refused to listen. It certainly didn't help his case to profess undying love for me yet refuse to let me anywhere near his family, who still assumed we were a summer fling and nothing more. I suspected he was ashamed of our pseudo-relationship because it would reflect poorly on him if it were uncovered that he, a respected Catholic, was pursuing a Jewish girl who wanted to be a rabbi.

Interestingly, John was able to see changes in my

character long before I could. When I tried to put an end to all the physical activity, he told me he didn't like the kind of person I was becoming. He thought I was "too conservative," and even fanatical, for taking God so literally. When I told him he was not the man I fell in love with anymore, he'd say the same thing right back to me: I was not the woman he loved (or claimed to love) anymore either. He claimed to still attend mass every Sunday, but his faith seemed compartmentalized into that one day of his life. Looking back, all the red flags seem so obvious, but I still had more heartache and growth to experience before mustering up the courage to break up for good.

Mainstream evangelicals seem to favor neatly boxed testimonies: open-and-shut moments when doubt is flushed away and the truth becomes perfectly clear. I don't have a testimony like that. Sure, I prayed the "sinner's prayer" like I was told to, but I don't mark that day in October, the fall semester of my sophomore year of college, as the day my life radically transformed. My story of faith is–and continues to be–a process where I learn a little more, backslide and contemplate giving up, take sabbaticals from prayer only to realize I miss God and come crawling back, and come close to brushing up against some truths while struggling to comprehend others.

Then there are some church groups who market Christianity as some kind of "get rich quick" fix, where all you have to do is believe and suddenly everything is perfect: the crumbling marriage leaning toward divorce, adult acne, disobedient children, the disagreeable boss. God gets reduced from an all-powerful Creator to a cosmic genie who dispenses fortune like soda from a vending machine.

I assumed the matter of "getting saved" would need to be carried out in a particular setting. I wondered if I should accept Jesus in the privacy of my own bedroom, or in an open grassy field–some peaceful place of solitude and majestic scenery. I couldn't just whisper in my head, "Hey Jesus let's be friends!" while rushing to get to class on time. This was all so new to me, and the friends I had who (supposedly) accepted Christ from the time they could toddle had done so in Church or in Sunday school. My impromptu approach to God, if you haven't already noticed, was definitely not the norm; but I was about to find a way to make it work.

If I'm going to be technical about it, I "accepted Christ as my personal Savior" (the phrase reeks of "Christian-ese" and makes me cringe a little every time I say it) on October 8, 2008–not in a grassy field or place of religious significance, but on the bathroom floor of my dorm. Not exactly ideal, but I didn't plan it that way. It happened one evening after a fight with John. I hung up the phone, went to the bathroom to splash cold water on my face, and started crying. I slumped to the floor, tucked my knees close to my chest and, while leaning against the door, I said out loud, "God, I can't keep living like this anymore."

I was tired of trying to make my buffet-style spirituality work, only to be continually frustrated. Earning salvation was not as simple as it seemed. I was tired of looking to other people to define God for me and tell me what was forbidden and what was permissible. I prayed to God for some kind of answer to it all, and consequently ended up praying for the first time to Jesus Christ.

Even if it wasn't a moment of crystal clarity for me, it was the moment a line was drawn in the sand: I officially handed over my Judaism in exchange for a life of heresy, as far as the Jewish community was concerned. But I was too wrapped up in anxiousness and desperation to consider the tectonic shifting of my soul that had just occurred. I just wanted some peace.

Life would surely be different now. At the very least of possibilities, I wanted the comfort of knowing I was on the right path after all. If I was lucky, maybe I'd even be more likeable (because I had the Holy Spirit now). Or just a carbon copy of Anne.

It rained hard the next day, and I was too tired to bother with getting up. Nor was I ready to face the world with something "different" about me. So I gave myself a mental health day and spent the majority of it in bed. Little did I know how turbulent and unpredictable the next few months would be. Since John and I were technically "on a break" while we were in school, and I still felt unbearably lonely, I went on a few dates with guys I knew were bad for me. I learned that I am not the sort of person who can give away pieces of herself without feeling cheapened, and I fell into depression.

But I didn't quit on God. I hounded him with

prayer after prayer after prayer, filling up my journal, but it seemed fitting that I should get another one because my prayer life was about to go in a whole new direction.

God showing up in people's lives like a stranger on your doorstep is not an uncommon theme in the bible. Whenever a drastic life event occurs, like Abraham making a covenant with God in Genesis, it usually warrants a name change. Before the covenant, Abraham was Abram, and his wife Sarai became Sarah.

I would sign my prayers as "Sarah Elizabeth," simply because my full name was such a mouthful and rarely ever used. What happened on the bathroom floor of my dorm (that sounds a bit dirty, doesn't it?) on October 8, 2008 was definitely a turning point. So from then on, in the style of the woman I was named for, I became "Sarahbeth."

It may seem silly, but it felt necessary.

10

While feasting on chicken wings and nachos at Applebee's one evening, I said to my friend Bethany, "Something very serious is happening, and I need to tell someone about it."

Her eyebrows raised with interest. "Oh?"

I stifled a laugh as she braced herself, like I was about to reveal that I was pregnant or that somebody had died. I wanted to dramatize this moment for all it was worth. "I think I'm falling in love with Jesus."

I hated to burst her bubble by telling her I wasn't converting to Catholicism (denominations are another playing field altogether) but suddenly we had a lot more in common. She told me I should check out Campus Crusade for Christ on campus to find community and explore some questions I might have. Imagine…roughly a year ago, I had completely written off that organization as nothing more than a shameful ploy to convert people. Now I was suddenly brimming with curiosity, but I begged her to come with me since I probably wouldn't know anyone.

Actually, I did know at least one person. By chance or divine planning, I came face to face with Stephanie: the girl who had sent me the email when I was a freshman about getting together for lunch, and whom I'd harshly chastised for wanting to convert me. I didn't recognize her at first, but she remembered my name and was so shocked to see me, the girl who wanted nothing to do with Jesus, *voluntarily* joining a meeting. She threw her hands in the air and proclaimed "God is good!" for everyone to hear. Then she gave me a hug.

Needless to say, I was so embarrassed. She said not to worry about it; she'd gotten much ruder responses than mine. That was good to know, I guess.

Joining Cru's weekly meetings was like stepping into an entirely different continent. The meetings were held in a lecture hall and were led by a young, enthusiastic staff team who coordinated social events (like movie nights, retreats, and holiday-themed parties) as well as the spiritual ones (like Summer Project, a missions-based volunteer program, and a missions trip to Rome every spring break). They took turns giving "talks" (the word "sermon" was a bit too formal for this crowd) about various subjects relating to the daily grind of college life. Growing up in my town, it was the "cool" thing to belong to a popular church, but these people took the definition of "Christian" to a whole new level: just going to church on Sundays or joining a bible study wasn't enough.

If there was any message that Crusade stressed the most, it was how to let one's faith permeate *every* aspect of one's life, not just one day a week. Who we are in fellowship shouldn't change when we return to our dorms, our classes, our jobs. We all have our own interests and our own priorities, they said, but God must be in the center of it all.

I appreciated their openness to questions, but there were many things I could not get used to–like the worship music at the end of every "talk." Cru didn't have just one guitar player, like Hillel did: they had a whole band, with the speakers turned up so loud the words were almost indecipherable. I quickly learned to avoid the rows of seats closest to the stage.

It was like the Holy Spirit literally took over the

people who sat quietly and serenely during the talks. With the opening chords of each song, they were jumping around, arms stretched out, waving and praising and putting their whole bodies into worship. This was a new experience, a part of a culture I knew nothing about, so I tried not to be judgmental. But honestly, the booming amps gave me a headache, some of the lyrics were downright cheesy, and the sea of people raising one arm while facing forward reminded me of a Hitler Youth rally–an unsettling feeling for a Jew who is new to church.

Over time I forced myself to learn the songs, but I couldn't get into them the same way everyone else could. I was so used to praying on my own, in my room with my journal, that I felt downright silly throwing my arms around. The few times I tried, I felt stiff and unauthentic. A friend of mine told me that worship isn't really worship if you're more concerned what everyone else thinks than focusing on God. I agree with him, which is why I am more comfortable worshiping in my own way. The temptation to put on a show disappears. I'm definitely more of a silent worshiper than a collectively-shout-sing-and-jump-around-the-room worshiper.

The fact that I was a "Jewish Christian" (that's what they called me) made me somewhat of a novelty. People wanting to get to know me and welcome me to the group were blown away by my "testimony" and insisted it was such a blessing to be Jewish and a believer in Jesus. It was flattering at first...and then it quickly became annoying, especially when some of my new friends expressed that they wished they had been raised as Jews, too.

They meant well, but clearly had no idea what they were talking about. So many of them had grown up in the church, in Christian families, and claimed to have gotten saved as toddlers. They had virtually no concept of what it meant to risk everything simply for believing something different. I was jealous of many girls in my bible study who seemed to have it all together (on the outside, anyway).

It wasn't until much later that I learned many of the "cradle Christians" of Cru experienced a season of rebellion between high school and college. Even for those who couldn't remember a time they weren't Christian, there was almost always a tempestuous middle.

One new friend told me how his mother, an atheist, flat-out told him she didn't love him anymore after he became a Christian. That was humbling: I felt bad for complaining about my situation, certain that my parents' love for me was unconditional even if they wouldn't give me their blessing for everything that I did. This friend wasn't trying to downplay my struggle; he was only giving me some perspective. In his case, his biological family was not his "true" family.

He told me, "Don't look at being Jewish as a stumbling block. It just means you have a story to tell." Those words, spoken with a quiet, gentle spirit after tasting rejection in its most bitter form, gave me the first inkling of hope I'd had in months.

The Cru staff is trained to help new Christians grow in their faith by getting them acquainted with older, more experienced "disciplers." However–and I can't say I blame them for this–they were completely unprepared to handle a new Christian like me. I imagine they don't receive too many of them who were raised Jewish, so they had no idea how to counsel me and reassure me that I wasn't a heretic.

It helped to have new supportive friends, but I still wanted my old ones (and my family) to stand behind me, too. I wanted to be honest and real about who I was, about how my life was changing. I hated saying hello to my Hillel friends on the way to class while tucking my cross necklace (a brave, impulsive purchase) underneath my shirt.

More than that, I wanted peace with myself. I wanted to know that who I was becoming and who I'd been could coexist peacefully.

Maybe God's "purpose" for me was to act as a bridge between these two faiths, which are both profoundly different but also profoundly similar.

In a bittersweet twist of fate, I started out "too Jewish" for my Catholic friends in elementary school, but not Jewish enough for the kids I met at summer camp, with their youth group logos and wristbands. In Israel, I didn't feel I had the right to call myself Jewish at all. Now I was too Christian for Jews everywhere, but still too Jewish to completely fit in with my new friends at Cru.

In my most pessimistic moments, I wonder if I'll

fit in anywhere, with anyone. It's interesting because Christians are called to be pariahs, to go against the ways of this world. But I am a special kind of pariah.

11

The next anniversary of my bat mitzvah was fast approaching: a day I fondly remember like my first awkward slow dance. While a tad misguided, Sarah Elizabeth was someone whose innocence and childlike faith I sorely envied, even if that faith was in homage to a god of her own devising, with slight Jewish undertones (yes, I do refer to my old self in the third person. I don't care if that's weird).

While I was struggling to fit both halves of my life together, I was introduced to someone who understood completely what I was going through.

One of the Cru staff members emailed me about a girl who was new to the campus, and was also–lo and behold–a new Christian from a Jewish family. Call this an experiment in divine friendship matchmaking.

The new girl's name was Natalie, and she was a freshman. I was told she was expecting to hear from me, so I sent her a message on Facebook introducing myself, asking if she would like to meet for coffee sometime. Within the hour, I received a response.

She wrote that almost no one understood what she was going through spiritually, and she took me up on my offer for coffee. When we met on campus that week, and I was blown away by how much we had in common. Her hometown was slightly more Jewish than mine (though not by much), and her family was pretty laid-back religiously. Also like me, she too stopped attending services after her bat mitzvah (though she didn't opt for the confirmation ceremony later).

The only difference between us–and it was a very crucial difference–was that she had already told her parents she was a Christian. Mine, as far as I knew, were still clueless. Mom acted like that conversation in the car had never happened, and probably assumed it was a phase or something, because I hadn't brought it up since.

I was jealous of Natalie's courage. She credited Cru for giving her the strength to talk about it with her parents and sisters. While I completely understood that telling your Jewish family you believed in Jesus was no cakewalk, she almost made it sound…too easy.

To be fair, it's not as if her family embraced her decision with open arms and said, "It's okay honey, whatever makes you happy." They didn't disown her, but they did tell her they thought she was making a big mistake. I imagined mine might react in a similar way.

Natalie became my lifeline in the following months, especially during the holiday season. We were like spiritual twins separated at birth. The problem was, as more time passed, Natalie seemed to want less and less to do with Judaism, to a point where she eventually decided she didn't need it altogether. I still kept going to Hillel every so often. I wasn't ready to give it up, nor did I plan to unless my presence there became a disturbance to others. Natalie attended a service or two with me, but seemed very removed from it all. Eventually I received this email: "SB, thanks so much for helping me out with everything, but I think the Jewish chapter of my life is closed and I honestly don't feel Jewish at all anymore. I think God is calling me to leave that part of my life behind. Sorry if that disappoints you."

Well, it certainly wouldn't be my place to argue what God was calling her to do with her life. At the same time, I wrote back asking if she was absolutely sure of what she was doing. "Think of the possibilities," I said, basically repeating everything my Cru friends had been telling me, in hopes that I could start believing it myself. "I really think you were born Jewish for a reason. Your Judaism could deepen your understanding of Christianity, and who knows how many more people like us are out there that you could help." In the end, her mind was made up: Judaism had failed her. But then again, hadn't it failed me as well? Why was I so offended by her decision?

While it's far more difficult to explain why Judaism is lost without Christianity, there's a whole world of reasons why Christians would be lost without Judaism–reasons I never discovered until I actually became one. Christians everywhere are in awe of Jesus the Savior, but first and foremost, I am inspired by Jesus the Jew. Jesus without Judaism is no Jesus at all.

It makes sense that the bible focuses mainly on

Jesus' life as an adult, when his ministry began. Not much is said about his life before that, which I find frustrating. I often wonder: what must it have been like to parent a kid like Jesus? Did he *ever* get into trouble? What kind of games did he play as a child? Moreover, I wonder if Mary, true to stereotype, was just as much of a nagger and a busybody as any Jewish mother (minus the New York accent). How might she have reacted if a neighborhood boy was picking on little Jesus? Did Joseph ever feel undermined in his role as an earthly father?

Not long after joining Campus Crusade for Christ, I removed the Star of David necklace I bought on my first trip to Israel. I never left the house without it; removing it felt like an amputation. No, worse: a true sign of crossing over enemy lines. Still, I couldn't shake feelings of dishonesty and treason the more I continued to wear the star–like I was lying to everyone who saw it. I used to only wear my cross to Cru meetings, but now it was time to be the real me everywhere I went.

Mom was the first to notice the Star of David's absence (I never wore the cross at home). There was no lecture; she simply stated, "You're not wearing your Star of David anymore." I just nodded and said something to the effect of "Nope, I'm not." That was it. Conversation ended. I asked what we were having for dinner.

Then a funny thing happened on my twentieth birthday: she gave me a new necklace–a silver heart with the words from Psalm 27, "The Lord is My Light" engraved on it. A verse both Christians *and* Jews can believe in. That became my new "default" necklace for a while, and it made me hopeful. It felt like a little symbol from heaven that everything was going to work out just fine with my family.

The fall semester of sophomore year was coming to a close, and I was three quarters of the way done with my mandatory foreign language class. Not surprisingly, since I wanted to be a rabbi at the start of my freshman year, the language I chose was Hebrew. I'd had no reason to study it since my ninth grade confirmation, so my comprehension skills were more than a little rusty. It was easier to study when I thought I needed to learn it for my career. Now I really had to force myself to pay attention and stay motivated. At that point, all I wanted was just to get it done.

Earlier in the semester I had a solid B+. A month or so into the class, it dropped to a B- when I didn't do so well on the midterm. By the time finals came around, my grade was a solid C+.

When the anniversary of my Bat Mitzvah came around again, I wasn't sure how to define what I was feeling. It didn't help that, on that date, Hillel was hosting a talk with a local rabbi on why it isn't Jewish to believe Jesus is the Messiah. I considered attending, so long as I could promise myself to keep my mouth shut; I just wasn't in the mood to be ripped to shreds by anyone who might be horribly offended by my presence. But I knew it wouldn't be possible for me to do that. So I stayed at home and, like a good little heathen, did Hebrew homework instead.

12

Being disqualified from rabbi-hood left me dry in the career department. Therefore, the right thing to do would be to drop out of the Jewish Studies program I was minoring in. While one need not be Jewish to minor in the program, I felt unethical about continuing to receive scholarship money from it.

I have to admit, I do miss the shock on people's faces when they'd ask about my career plans. Now all I can say is "I'm not sure what I want to do, but I'll figure it out eventually"–just like every other person in the millennial generation. I lost something that used to make me stand out. It may sound absurd, but there was a grieving process I needed to go through.

My dropping out of the Jewish Studies program didn't go unnoticed for long. Because there were so few people in it, rumors started to spread, and some of the friendly faces I was accustomed to at Hillel didn't appear so friendly anymore. Only a few people asked me why I dropped out, but the way they asked suggested they already knew the answer. I explained that I had changed my mind about careers, so I no longer needed the minor, which was the truth (or at least a part of it).

My conversion was one thing; my involvement with Cru, the most influential evangelical group on campus, was another matter (I guess it doesn't help that the organization's name is an obvious reference to *the* Crusades in the Middle Ages). One Hillel friend, as part of an assignment for her comparative religion class, attended a Cru meeting to take notes. I panicked, just slightly, when I saw her sitting two rows behind me. Before I could think of what to say, she chirped, "Doesn't all this preachy talk bother you? *So* glad Jews don't have to deal with that." A naturally chatty girl, she went on to tell me about the class, and I kept nodding like a bobblehead doll because it prevented me from having to open my mouth.

Facebook was another big incriminator regarding my weekly Christian activities. I subscribed to Cru's Facebook group to keep up to date on all the latest events. But privacy is a privilege you can never expect on a social networking site, and in a cowardly way I was grateful for that. Having people find out about my conversion via Internet saved me from having to muster the courage to confess it out loud.

I was well aware (and in some cases, paranoid) that more of my Jewish friends were starting to treat me differently. I told myself to get over it; that I simply wasn't important enough to be the center of any major scandal. No one was rude to me or outright questioned me about hanging with Cru (at least not yet), but I could have sworn there was something icy in a few people's voices when they greeted me on Friday nights at Hillel.

I quickly found I had another big bone to pick with Christianity as a Jew: evangelism. Oh, how evangelists bothered me. I resented not being able to walk to class at times without having some visiting preacher (they came frequently to my liberal party school) thrusting a pamphlet in my face, with bright red letters screaming "TURN OR BURN!" The audacity of some evangelists I've seen over the years just appalled me. And now that I, too, was Christian, evangelism suddenly became my responsibility. I just knew there was a catch somewhere. With Judaism, there were kosher laws. With Christianity, evangelism.

I would have rather given up cheeseburgers.

Weekly Cru meetings didn't turn me into a sign-carrying preacher with a bullhorn on a sidewalk corner. In the staff's defense, this is what they had to say about it: if you talked about Jesus to bolster your own superiority complex, you were doing it wrong. Evangelism–or as they called it, "sharing your faith"–is supposed to be an act of love. Christians should talk about Jesus the way most people talk about their significant others. I was supposed to gush about Jesus the same way I raved about *The Hunger Games* and Jane Austen.

Okay, I guess I could get on board with that.

In my experience, evangelism is done best when it is lived, not just preached. The gospel is supposed to transform one's life in such a way that others can't help but notice. At the same time, if I'm seen helping an elderly woman cross the street, or donating large sums of money to charity, no one will immediately assume it's because I have Jesus in my heart.

I just kept thinking of Anne, who lived out the gospel message more authentically than anyone I'd ever met. There was no secret formula or catchy pamphlet slogans with her. She just loved Jesus, and that love was manifested in everything she said or did.

Now that the gospel was condensed into bite-sized pieces so I could (kinda sorta) understand it, putting the message into action was another challenge. I can't lie here–I was terrified of rejection, especially from the people my Cru friends thought needed to hear it most: my parents.

The older girls who took me under their wing told me gently, albeit sternly, that I needed to tell my unbelieving parents about Jesus–sooner rather than later. My dad apparently needed to hear it more, being a rebound cancer patient and all. "You just never know when the Lord might call him home, you know," they would tell me, as casually as "Can you pass the chips?" I broke out in a cold sweat at the thought of saying to my Jewish parents, "Hey Mom and Dad, do you mind sitting down so I can share the gospel with you?" Yeah, that would go over real well.

I don't know why I wasn't furious with those girls for being so insensitive. I guess I really thought they were only trying to help me.

"Just pray that the Holy Spirit will give you courage," they said. "God will protect you!" they said.

Maybe they meant well, but they had no damn clue about reality. What they ended up doing was nearly scaring all the Jesus out of me, because if I wasn't brave enough to confess my belief before my parents, how would I survive the Tribulation?

Truth be told, I felt more Jewish surrounded by gentiles than I ever did around other Jews.

My friend Bethany was convinced she had a foolproof method of breaking "the news" to my unsuspecting parents. "Just tell them that you're pregnant," she advised. "But before they can fall over in shock, that's when you say 'Just kidding! I'm not pregnant, I'm just a Christian.'" Ideally, they'd be so relieved that I wasn't pregnant, believing in Jesus wouldn't seem so bad.

I *wish* it were only an out-of-wedlock pregnancy I had to tell them about. That would have made my life much easier.

I started to have this reoccurring dream, clearly foreshadowing my "coming out" to the world as a Christian. In the dream, I was wearing a cross necklace I kept tucking under my shirt every time I passed a Jewish friend or family member. Just like Pinocchio's nose every time he told a lie, the cross grew bigger every time I became self-conscious of it, to a point where I just couldn't hide it anymore…and eventually everyone saw me for what I really was.

I would wake up in the morning feeling sweaty, sickened, and depressed once more.

13

Here's one thing I still can't do as a Christian: say "Merry Christmas" to strangers over "Happy Holidays." I just know better, since it wasn't that long ago I used to bristle at having received dozens upon dozens of Merry Christmases, but one or two Happy Hanukkahs out of the whole season. *The whole damn season.*

I've always enjoyed Christmas–or at least the secular Americanized version of it. There is something undeniably magical about the lights, the carols, the seasonal salted caramel mochas from Starbucks with extra salt around the rim of the cup. I'd help my friends decorate their trees, and in turn they would come over to my house for latkes and candle lighting.

As a new Christian, though, I have to say: there is just no substitute for a drinking game of dreidel.

My first Hanukkah as a Christian fell during finals week, but Hillel hosted a Hanukkah party the weekend before. While feasting on latkes, Rachel, my former Hebrew tutor, asked me how rabbinical plans were going. When I told her that my plans had changed (but not the reason why), what happened next was like a perfect sitcom moment–everyone within earshot who knew me as Sarah the Future Rabbi looked positively stunned, and there was a simultaneous dropping of the forks (okay, that last part didn't actually happen, but let's just pretend it did).

For a moment, I felt like I'd personally betrayed Rachel, who began tutoring me my senior year of high school. I wondered if she thought all our hard work had been flushed down the drain. When she asked what made me change my mind, I had no idea how to answer. Sure, there was the option of telling the truth, but a Hanukkah party didn't feel like the right atmosphere for a potential debate on why Judaism and Jesus don't mix. I stuttered and fumbled to find the right words, but all I could come up with was, "Um, well, I don't know anyone who sticks to the same career choice they made when they were fifteen."

I don't think she was totally satisfied by that answer. But good old Bethany, my Catholic friend checking out her first Hanukkah party, saved me by piping up "You know, when I was fifteen I wanted to be a middle school teacher, but when I got to college I realized I work better with younger children. So I switched my concentration to early childhood education." This prompted a girl across the table to reply, "Hey, that's exactly what I did!" The mood of the conversation changed entirely, and Bethany leaned over to whisper in my ear, "I just saved your butt, you know." She was definitely right about that.

When I went back home for holiday break (*not* Christmas break, thank-you-very-much!), Bethany invited me to go caroling at a nursing home with Saint Catherine's youth group. After my participation in the town Christmas pageant as a child, this was another activity my mother had no problem with ("It's just singing, right?"). Other than that, I wasn't sure what else I should be doing to observe my first official Christmas. I felt awkward popping into a local church for one day only–especially when I knew I could run into someone I went to high school with. I just didn't feel like explaining why I was there, by myself, and clearly unaware of what to expect from a traditional Christmas service.

Other than going out for the traditional Chinese dinner and movie with my family, I decided to observe in my own way by reading the opening chapters of the Gospel of Luke, which describe Christ's birth. Then I rented *The Nativity Story* and watched it Christmas Eve, long after the rest of the house went to sleep. It was celebratory enough for me, even if all my friends were getting dressed to the nines for midnight Mass with their families. I could never get into the standard Christian films my friends loved growing up, like *A Christmas Carol* or *It's a Wonderful Life*. I hated them as a kid because they made me feel left out, so I have a hard time enjoying them as an adult.

Someday, I will attend a Christmas Eve service—but not before having a feast of Chinese food. Otherwise it just wouldn't be right.

14

My heart literally skipped a beat when I went to Hillel one Friday night and saw there was a brand new hostess…*wearing a Star of David necklace with a cross in the middle.*

Was I in the wrong building? Did Kent State decide to build a Jews for Jesus Church-agogue? Why on earth would Hillel hire someone whose taste in jewelry could be bad for business?

Hoping to God she was another spiritual twin, I ran up to her and introduced myself.

As it turned out, Danielle is not a Christian. She wears that necklace to honor her interfaith parents and mixed upbringing, but she asked to have a bat mitzvah and is decidedly Jewish. Still, her open-mindedness encouraged me. She had a great sense of humor when people stiffened at the sight of that necklace; some even demanded to know why she was wearing it (a few years ago I probably would have done the same thing). If Hillel had no problem with it, maybe I could still belong there after all.

At the same time, I knew I had to prepare to lose a few friends. It would hurt, but isn't it always better to be disliked for who you are than loved for who you are not? The only approval I cared about was that of my family. Everyone else…well, I'd say they could go to hell, but that's not very tactful.

I knew my mother was growing more suspicious, but still she did not say anything about it. When spring semester began, I decided I would avoid going home on weekends for a while, for as long as it would take to prepare what I was going to say.

Somehow I made it through holiday break in one piece, but not without a few breakdowns and desperate phone calls to Bethany late at night. I didn't feel comfortable calling Natalie. Our friendship was straining because of her unwillingness to have anything to do with Judaism and my not-so-subtle disagreement with that. I was so jealous of her for already telling her family, it hurt.

My Cru bible study met every Monday evening in the downstairs lounge of the dining hall. It's a popular place for people to study, and as fate would have it, one day I noticed a girl from Hillel sitting across from us–the same girl who'd tried to hook me up with that "You're too Jewish for me" kid my freshman year (I hadn't forgotten!).

My former matchmaker's pupils blew up to the size of golf balls as the girls opened their bibles. Then…then…*she started walking toward us.*

I wanted to laugh the first time I heard a Christian talk about being persecuted–at least in America. It was so difficult not to retort "Oh please. Your religion dominates everything in this country. You have no idea what 'persecution' is!" But in that moment I wondered if situations like this were what they were referring to…that moment when public displays of faith made you look like a crazy person.

"Seriously?" she asked.

My throat dried up, so I could only manage a nod in response.

"Well," she sighed, "I guess there's nothing wrong with learning about other religions."

My voice decided to make a miraculous comeback. "Actually, we're reading the book of Micah," I explained.

She just stared at me, confused. "It's from the Old Testament," I clarified.

"Oh." She shrugged, not really caring one way or the other. "Well, have fun."

She walked away, and we never spoke again.

I relayed that incident to my friend Melissa when she drove me home from a Cru meeting one rainy night. "Maybe I shouldn't have said anything, just to avoid a conflict," I lamented. "I don't think I owe anyone an explanation for what I believe, and I don't want to start any—"

Once she pulled up to the entrance of my dorm, Melissa abruptly put the car into park so she could look me square in the eye. "SB, you know what I think?" I figured she was going to tell me even if I said no; I didn't want to know, so I just nodded. She repeated my own metaphor back to me: "You need to get out of the spiritual closet already."

It actually gave me a dose of courage to hear another person say that.

I still felt inadequate at Cru, surrounded by Christians who had been Christians since diapers. But outside of that, when I met new people who knew nothing of my past, the cross I wore gave the impression that I was a "cradle Christian" as well.

On the first day of Sociology class my junior year, I arrived a few minutes early. Selecting a seat at the back of the auditorium, I quietly read my bible. Soon I was interrupted by a tap on my shoulder and a voice that chirped, "Whatcha readin'?"

This intrusion by a complete stranger felt rude and startling. Upon turning around, I'm embarrassed to say my annoyance quickly evaporated when I saw that the person who interrupted me was a *guy*, and he happened to be quite attractive. From the get-go, he assumed I was *one of those* nerdy Jesus Freaks. He nicknamed me "Christian Nerd," which eventually got shortened to just "Nerd." I couldn't come up with any clever nicknames for him so I just called him by his given name: Ryan.

Every day he would sit next to me, and every day he would greet me with, "What's up, Nerd? Save any souls lately?" I always brushed him off, but was oddly flattered that my spiritual devotion was recognized in such a way that didn't make him want to run in the opposite direction. When I used to tell people I wanted to be a rabbi, one of two things would happen next: they would be very interested and want to know more, or wonder what planet I just landed from.

Ryan seemed to have me all figured out within the first week of class. He thought I was from a family of devout Christian Republicans who home-schooled me, forbid me to wear makeup, listen to secular music, go on dates, or see any movie rated higher than PG.

I didn't have the heart to tell him I was descended from a long line of liberal Jews who *always* voted Democrat, drank, cursed, and believed the only unforgiveable sin was rooting against the New York Yankees.

He was funny at first, but the constant heckling about my apparent prude-like ways was starting to get old fast.

Then one day he asked for my number, which led

to asking me out for lunch after class. I let his good looks get in the way of my good judgment by saying yes.

Meeting for lunch at Wendy's after class became a tradition, until one day he informed me that, while I was cute and all, he didn't see me as a potential girlfriend because I was…wait for it…*too Christian for him*.

From "too Jewish" to "too Christian" in the span of a single year. Go figure.

15

First, there was a girl wearing a cross at Hillel. Then, there was Emily–the quirky yet likeable girl who wore a Star of David at Cru. I could see it glinting on her shirt as she spoke about an upcoming mission trip to Brazil. *Is that a…? Why yes, yes it is!*

I *had* to meet her. I'd been asking God to send me signs of hope, and here he was sending me a billboard!

Up close I could see that inside her star was the Hebrew name for Jesus, *Yeshua*. When I told her a little about myself, she threw her arms around me and declared I was her new best friend. We were inseparable for the few weeks up until she left for her trip. *Of course God answered my prayer with a wrench thrown into it,* I thought. However, this is why he invented email and Skype. We would communicate as often as possible. She wrote that she was constantly praying for me and my family, and sent me bible verses to give me the strength I would need when I talked to them eventually.

When she returned, I had the really dumb idea of

introducing her to Natalie. At first I thought how cool it would be if the three of us could form a little Christians-Who-Were-Raised-Jewish club or something. But I decided not to. I hadn't spoken to Natalie in months, and she'd made no effort to try and bridge the gap. Regretfully, I let her go.

Emily, on the other hand, was dying to check out Hillel. If Danielle managed just fine with her cross-inside-the-star necklace, Emily should be okay. She was such a trooper, introducing herself and shaking everyone's hands. During the service, she chanted perfect Hebrew with her eyes squeezed shut, as if to say to any potential naysayers "See, I'm just as Jewish as all of you. I don't need no English transliteration!" I was so proud of her for simply being herself, for letting her little light shine. I wondered how it got to be so easy for her when it seemed next to impossible for me to do the same.

At the end of the night, as she drove me back to my dorm, she told me she had a little confession to make: apparently she wasn't raised Jewish like I originally thought. She was raised in a Christian home, but several years ago her family joined a

Messianic synagogue, and would I like to go sometime?

Okay, I admit. I felt a *little* cheated. But a Messianic synagogue? That existed? It sounded as odd as a vegan slaughterhouse, but I told her I'd think about it.

16

If I thought I was being tested already, more surprises were yet to come. As summer break drew closer, Mom informed my brother and I that a family trip back to Israel was in the works. Dad was the healthiest he'd ever been after several months of chemo, and had the approval from his doctor to travel. Since we never knew how long each period of remission would last, Mom went ahead and booked the trip.

Anyone else would have been thrilled. As soon as I found out, I burst into tears. I sought every possible method to avoid it: getting a job, nrolling in summer school… *anything*. It was bad enough visiting as a pick-and-choose Jew. Now as a Jew-turned-Christian, I simply wasn't ready to go back. Maybe in a year or two, but definitely not that summer. And not with my *family,* who, as far as I knew, still had no clue who I really was.

But because it was a family trip, I had to go. Of course I was expected to go.

Two weeks in the Holy Land would not kill me, I

decided. Think how jealous my Cru friends would be! If nothing else, I'd have some cool pictures to post on Facebook and fun stories to tell.

But in the weeks leading up to the trip, I flipped back and forth between excitement and panic. It should have been easier to feel excited when everyone else was excited, but I couldn't. Once I got desperate and said to Mom, *"But what about the terrorists??"* She stared me down and said, "If you live your life in fear, SB, you won't live at all."

In light of everything else, it was impossible to argue that logic.

The trip was organized so that we never stayed in the same hotel for longer than two days. We rented a van, forcing us all into closer proximity than what was healthy or sane. Not only that, my brother's friend Erica from his youth group somehow ended up traveling with us, resulting in even *less* legroom and even *less* privacy–already a scarcity for any family vacation.

Erica, as it turned out, was *not* a fan of Christians. While everyone else was keen on touring the Church of the Holy Sepulchre, built on the spot where Jesus was crucified, she fiercely objected. Even my brother protested, "Come on, it's historically interesting," but she merely scoffed at how totally unfair it was for Christians to infiltrate on the Jewish homeland.

I wanted to point out that the earliest Christians were Jews, but I bit my tongue. She was one eye-roll away from getting the snot beaten out of her.

Then, at a midday lunch stop, she randomly mentioned someone she knew back home who was now, apparently, a "Jew for Jesus," and that made her sick. No one said anything in response. My appetite gone, I pushed my food around my plate, trying to keep my composure. What was this girl's *problem*? She had to suspect something, somehow, because these comments felt too deliberate and personal.

It wasn't even a full week since we'd arrived in Israel. Why did I let myself get dragged here, again?

The best–and worst–parts were still to come, if you can believe it. One day, while meandering through the markets of the Arab quarter, I passed a display of necklaces with symbols I had never seen before: a menorah attached to a Star of David, attached to the Christian fish symbol. I didn't know this was called the Messianic Seal of Jerusalem, an ancient symbol found on Mount Zion.

I was only looking–I didn't even have much money on me–when suddenly I saw the shadow of my mother creeping behind me, and her voice was icy enough to frost a cake: "You can't buy that."

The hairs on the back of my neck stood up on end, despite it being a hundred degrees even under the tent of the market. "I was just–"

She held her hand up to stop me. "You can't buy one of those. Everyone will want to see what you bought. It's going to upset them and…" She stopped herself when she noticed my face, reddened with the embarrassment of being "caught" (a different kind of redness than comes from being out in intense desert heat).

She knew. My mother knew. Now that the façade was lifted, I tried to explain that no one would have to see it, that necklaces are small and I could easily hide it in my purse and no one would have to know

I'd made a purchase, but what would be the point of that? It's not like I could safely wear it anywhere.

It's completely loony tunes, but I started having dreams about that necklace: I would be shopping by myself and see an immaculate display of those Seals, only to have them evaporate into thin air when I reached out to touch them. I knew these dreams were not the root of a desire for yet another piece of jewelry, since God knows I have more than enough. This was definitely something deeper–perhaps a way to affirm who and what I had become, and validate it somehow. I'm not entirely sure.

The last thing I wanted to do was cause a disturbance and upset my mother, but I really, really, *really* wanted that necklace. Just because. Buying it would be a small, significant step in conquering my fear of what other people thought of me. I doubted I'd ever wear it, but that didn't matter.

From then on, Mom watched me like a hawk every time we shopped for trinkets. When my eyes lingered a moment too long at a jewelry display, she would sigh heavily in a way that indicated it was time to move on. While Greg and Erica went off on their own to look for souvenirs, Mom tailed me. I tried walking faster, hoping she'd get the message because I wasn't brave enough to just say, *"Please let me shop in peace!"* It would seem far too obvious, since we both knew what, specifically, I was shopping for.

The heat became unbearable as my stress level kept rising. My skin was sticky with sunscreen and sweat; my long skirt clung to my legs. Claustrophobia kicked in with so many tourists around me–let alone my mother following so closely behind.

I'd never had a panic attack before, but I think I started having one then. Now, finally, my "dirty little secret" was starting to unravel. I needed more time, but apparently God did not see fit to give me any. And of all the places in the world for my true identity to be revealed, it just had to be in the Holy Land. Go figure.

Like a true warrior, I cried in the taxi all the way back to the hotel. In an episode of pure déjà vu, I collapsed on the bathroom floor of our hotel room. It wasn't long before I heard a knock on the door, and my mother's voice on the other side: "Family meeting. Right now."

No questions asked. With my face still red and eyes still wet, I followed her out into the room where my father and brother were waiting. The last time I had seen them looking so serious at a "family meeting" like this was when Dad had something cancer-related to tell us.

They all sat on the bed, and I in a chair in front of them. I was on trial, sitting before not one, but *three* judges. My knees trembled; I closed my eyes and waited for the "meeting" to begin. The only blessing was Erica's absence. She must have been bribed to disappear for a while. *Baruch Hashem! Thank God.*

"Look," my mother began. "We all know you're experiencing a…*spiritual crisis.*" They all knew? That was news to me.

"And we're not exactly thrilled about it. But…" This was it. I clenched my fists, waited for them to tell me they were leaving me in Israel, that the Sanhedrin was waiting outside for me, stones in hand. "We thought you should know that we love you anyway."

I exhaled the breath I didn't realize I'd been holding until then. Blinking back more tears, I looked up. Did I hear her right? Was everything really going to be okay?

I don't know how long we sat in uncomfortable silence, but it was Dad who broke the ice and told me this would be a major adjustment to our family dynamic, and the "new normal" would not happen for a while. But hey, this was a very promising start.

"Just promise us one thing," said my mother. Once again I held my breath, expecting a Catch-22. *You can only be a Christian if you don't go to church* or something ludicrous like that. "Yes?" My voice was small and barely audible.

"Promise us you'll never vote Republican," they said.

We went to the market one last time before the end of the trip. This time I was allowed to wander by myself, but I was still cautious. When I passed by a jewelry display, I looked to my left, and didn't see anyone. I looked to my right, and the rest of the gang was looking at postcards. *The coast was clear.*

I got the attention of the woman behind the counter and pointed at a silver Seal pendant. It didn't appear that she knew much English, but even with hardly any words spoken, I think she somehow understood that this process was supposed to be urgent. She took the charm, wrapped it up in tissue paper, and pressed it into my hand at the same time I plunked down the right amount of shekels on the counter. The wrapped-up necklace went into my pocket, and I walked away. The exchange went down like an illegal drug deal, but it was done. I had no idea when, where, or *if* I'd ever wear the necklace, but the mission was accomplished, and that was all that mattered.

17

So my Jewish family found out I became a Christian, and the world did not end. But it was still a topic to be avoided: the non-kosher elephant in the room.

I tried to be understanding and imagine it from my parents' point of view. Of course this was hard for them. We just needed more time to adjust, and everything would be fine.

I think my family's biggest concern about me being a Christian was that I'd transform from a meek, well-mannered girl into a fire-breathing, closed-minded, Scripture-spouting lunatic right before their eyes. Thanks to Judaism, I'm pretty sure I'm too grounded to ever cross over from faithful to fanatical territory. Still, I wanted some change in my life to be evident. I didn't want my family to think, "So she believes in Jesus now, big deal. We thought we wouldn't recognize her anymore, but she still whines when it's her turn to take out the trash."

Yes, clearly there was still much progress to be made.

Sure enough, I returned to Cru's summer bible study with many stories to tell. But I wasn't the only person making a grand return home. I learned at Bethany's college graduation party that Anne had returned from the convent–possibly for good. That news really threw me off for some reason. After all, Anne was the one who had helped guide me through this difficult and confusing process of spiritual discovery. How could it be that her vocation was falling apart as well?

I guess I needed to hear the whole story first. She'd given away her cell phone, so the best way to get a hold of her was to go to the next mass with Bethany.

Before I had the chance to see her, I had coffee with Luke, my friend in the seminary. When I told him the news about my new Christian faith, I don't think he believed me at first. He had sufficient reason to doubt my intentions: I was still in love with John, but John's family didn't like my Jewishness. Ergo, I became a Christian.

I assured him that wasn't true.

It was weeks before I got to see Anne again. By the time we met for coffee, Luke had already told her about my conversion. He also told me ahead of time what had changed Anne's mind about being a nun: basically, at the tender age of twenty-two, she realized that she was too young and inexperienced in her faith to make such a drastic decision about convent life. Her fellow sisters at the convent were in full agreement on this. She didn't want there to be any doubts when she took her final vows. Even more than that, she now felt that God might be calling her to be a wife and a mom (in that exact order, of course).

She was still devoutly Catholic, but she was not Anne the Future Nun anymore; nor was I Sarah the Future Rabbi. The old joke about the priest, the nun, and the rabbi had fallen apart. Once again, there was some grieving involved.

18

After much begging, pleading, and offers of bribery, I finally accepted Emily's offer to visit her Messianic Synagogue, for no other reason except to get her off my back.

I had no idea what to expect, but I was skeptical. Would it be a normal evangelical service with traditional hymns, but with a side dash of Hebrew? Would the preacher simply don a *talit* and *yarmulke* and consider that Jewish enough? What if I hated it…or worse, what if I ended up *liking* it?

I was *especially* irritated at having to get up early on a Saturday for it–yep, the Jewish Sabbath. But Emily, darn that charm of hers, talked me into it by promising me Starbucks on the way. There's hardly anything I wouldn't do for Starbucks.

The first thing I noticed, once inside, were the women: they looked considerably Orthodox with their mid-length shirts and long skirts. Some even wore head coverings. The men wore suits and *talits* draped over their shoulders, all decked out with the same Messianic Seal I was wearing around my neck

(I figured that was the most acceptable place to wear it).

The service opened with the same Hebrew chants I knew by heart. I'll try not to be too judgmental here, but I have to confess: it did bother me that the rabbi (Minister? Preacher? What is the proper title for a Messianic Jewish leader?) kept mispronouncing certain words. *Aha!* I thought. *You must be a gentile, too!* But I wisely kept my mouth shut. The thing was, I could force my mouth shut or my mind to stay open, but it was *really* hard to do both. You'd think I would feel right at home in a place like this, but everything from the Israeli flag at the podium–next to a cross–to interspersing prayers with enthusiastic cries of *Yeshua HaMoshiach!* just felt…forced.

I wanted the seams of my identity to blend nicely with the rest of the fabric, but this was not the way to do it. This felt like a child forcing a puzzle piece into a space it didn't belong. I don't know how else to explain it.

It's tradition to kiss your prayer book and then touch the Torah with it as it is carried down the aisle mid-service, so as not to soil it with grimy human hands. But the Torah was being lifted from the Ark just after singing a song about Jesus. For some reason, as much as I believed in Christianity, I could not touch the Torah with my prayer book after that. That seemed like way more heresy than I could handle, and I already handled quite a lot.

There was even a rendition of *Hava Nagila*, a song and dance number usually reserved for weddings or bat mitzvahs, at the end. It was truly an effort in self-control not to groan out loud–like, how many Jewish traditions can you squeeze into one service?

This wasn't Jewish. This felt Jew-*ish*.

But it meant a lot to Emily, whom I liked and respected. When she asked what I thought, I told her "It was interesting," and left it at that.

I've met many Christians who use the phrases "Jew for Jesus" and "Messianic Jew" interchangeably, not realizing they are two completely different groups. Jews for Jesus is an evangelism campaign founded in 1973 by a man named Moishe Rosen–a Jewish-born Baptist preacher. Messianic Judaism is a unique branch of Christianity that initially began as a safe haven for Jews who believe in Jesus. Its popularity has grown due to a surplus of Protestants developing an interest in their faith's Jewish roots (2,000 years belated, in my opinion). This "denomination" now boasts a growing number of gentiles, like Emily, who want to see the Church return to her Jewish roots.

I agree that it is completely necessary for pastors to educate their congregants about Judaism, but I have many mixed feelings about the Messianic way of doing it. I love Chinese food, but I wouldn't be fooling anyone by calling myself Chinese. I can't help feeling the same way about Christians who "feel Jewish" because they love Judaism.

I recently bought a ring with the Yiddish word *bashert* engraved on it. Traditionally, *bashert* has been used on wedding bands and is interpreted as "soulmate." An additional interpretation is also "meant to happen," which I'd like to believe is an appropriate summary of my spiritual journey. Jesus refers to the Church as his bride in the Scriptures. No matter what label I call myself, Jesus is my *bashert*.

19

As a college senior, it was now my role to minister to Cru's incoming freshmen. After listening to the first few talks of the semester, I couldn't help thinking, *I've heard this all before.* The gospel message stayed the same, as it should have, but I did not feel I was learning anything new. That's when the shocking realization came to me: had I surpassed the 'baby Christian' stage already? It seems strange to think you can outgrow a place of worship, but that's exactly what I felt was happening. I guess it's not too surprising: the meltdown on the bathroom floor, when I first prayed to Jesus, had happened two years before.

The thought of leaving Cru in search of another church felt like spiritual adultery–especially after *finally* acquiring my first and only Christian T-shirt. It was actually nothing exciting–charcoal gray with "Cru at Kent" in blue block letters on the front. No catchy slogans. But you know what? The shirt didn't matter anymore. I didn't know for sure where I belonged, but my identity is in God, not people.

Now, it was time to find a new church home. The

only thing standing against me was time: it was my last year of college, and I worried I wouldn't find the right one in time. My concerns, however, were unfounded. God knew what he was doing, and what he did was creatively lead me to another spiritual home that would change my life: a campus church called h2o (yes, like water).

The story of how I met and fell in love with h2o Church begins with a story of how I met and became friends with one of its members: Patrick. After meeting in the Student Center through a mutual friend, and discovering that we lived in the same residence hall, Patrick and I bonded over a mutual love of C.S. Lewis. We spent hours discussing his books, our "testimonies," and our families. Eventually he convinced me I just *had* to check out his awesome church, which gathered in the same lecture hall that Cru did, but on Sunday evenings, not Thursdays (imagine my horror at the thought of becoming a Sunday churchgoer!).

Once again, I was bribed with an offer of free Starbucks. "This," I said to Patrick before I set foot in the door, "feels like spiritual adultery. Again." He simply rolled his eyes and told me to get over it.

At h2o, I was given the privilege of starting over. I was not Sarah-the-Jew-who-just-became-a-Christian. I was simply Sarahbeth, a curious college girl looking to join a new church. The staff was kind and welcoming. The other members, most of them freshmen and sophomores, hugged me as if I'd been attending forever. I was starting to get hooked–but not yet. I still needed to hear the sermon.

I nearly fell out of my seat when the pastor (yes, in this campus ministry there were pastors, not just "staff") started talking about the Jewish aspects of Jesus, and why Christians needed to learn more of the Old Testament. Patrick, who looked like he was trying hard to hold in his laughter, shot me a look that said *See? I told you you'd love it*. Who would have thought it would require a pastor talking about the the Old Testament to win me over to a new church?

What I loved most about h2o was that the Old Testament was discussed *frequently*. I couldn't recall ever hearing a talk about the Old Testament at Cru. h2o wasn't trying to merge two religions into one, or make the services Jewish; it simply explained Christianity as it already is: a religion born from Judaism.

Patrick was right: I was in love (with the church, I mean. Not him).

20

Two months into my membership at h2o, I took Communion. Not the Eucharist, as Catholics know it. I haven't made up my mind about whether the bread and wine (or crackers and grape juice, in this scenario) is the literal body and blood of Christ, but as students filed one by one to the stage, I decided to join them.

As the semester progressed, I made new friends and joined a new bible study. I also earned a position as an opinion columnist for the campus newspaper, which I was really excited about. Then, shortly after my twenty-second birthday, it was announced after a service that h2o was going to have a baptism ceremony. Anyone could sign up to be baptized, which stunned me: it was yet another tradition I assumed to be strictly Catholic domain.

For h2o, baptism was a public declaration of faith and commitment, not unlike a public declaration of wedding vows. The Holy Spirit must have been fast at work, because I raised my hand when the staff asked if anyone was interested.

The baptism took place in early December. At

first, I was confused: they wouldn't have us jump into a freezing lake as some kind of endurance test, would they? Was there a baptismal fount hidden underneath the lecturing stage or something?

Nope, the baptisms would take place in the pool at the campus recreational gym. No bikinis, just a T-shirt and gym shorts.

I was told ahead of time that I would have to prepare a brief testimony to share before getting dunked. By this point in time, most people were aware of my Jewish background–but the last thing I wanted to do was talk about it at my baptism. As I'm sure you know by now, my testimony is anything but *brief*. More importantly, the biggest reason I didn't want to talk about it was because I didn't think I could without crying.

I would be crying about how I never worked up the courage to tell my parents about my baptism. I would be crying after seeing the joyous faces of other students' parents and relatives who would be there to celebrate, knowing that for my family, this would not be an occasion worth celebrating.

I'm not proud of the fact that I never told them. In

fact, Patrick lectured me about it, pointing out the obvious fact that my parents already *know* I am a Christian; how shocking could a baptism be? If anything, they'd probably expect it. But I never told them. They found out about it eventually, as parents always do. They found out through the pictures that surfaced on Facebook within a week after the event. I had no idea there would be a photographer cataloging everyone's waterlogged faces as they emerged from the water. I know it was cowardly to have my parents find out that way, but regardless of how they did, I'm glad that they know.

I did give a statement about being baptized as a public declaration of faith, which is significant because the words "I am a Christian!" had rarely left my mouth before. I explained that I was done with hiding and being ashamed. With that, I jumped into the pool and was baptized in the name of the Father, the Son, and the Holy Spirit.

I emerged from the water as a new creation, and later that week, I went to the Summit County Court House and filed a request to make Sarahbeth my new legal name (with my parents' blessing). The first half, Sarah, obviously represents my Jewish heritage.

The second part, Beth, is the nickname of my new Christian self. But together, they are one.

21

My name change was declared legal by the state of Ohio in February of my senior year, but it was "official" in my eyes long before that. No one called me Sarah anymore (a name I never liked anyway), and I truly did feel like a new creation. With graduation only a few months away, I had much to be hopeful for.

But those last few months weren't without the slightest bit of scandal. I became known for taking controversial views in my newspaper columns, since I chose to represent a conservative perspective on social issues at a very liberal school. I understood full well the risk I was taking, knowing it could cost me more friends. But I was committed to writing about issues that mattered to me, one of which was religious tolerance. I wrote that as a Christian, I would never force my beliefs on others. That being said, I wouldn't sit idly by and allow others to criticize those beliefs either.

Who would have thought that the single most scandalous line of that column was the one where Sarahbeth Caplin, the former Jew known as Sarah

Elizabeth, admitted she was now a Christian.

I was prepared for backlash, and that is exactly what I got. "You disgust me," wrote one student in an email. "One minute you were going off about how you wanted to be a rabbi, and now you're saying you're a Christian? Either you're a crappy journalist, or just ashamed of what you really are."

Mom called that day, asking if it was *really* necessary to "come out" in the school newspaper. I told her yes, it absolutely was necessary. It showed me who my true friends were.

The next life-changing trial of faith was yet to come. As John, whom I never stopped loving from afar, kept asking if I was *sure* I didn't still want to hook up in secret, he also let it slip that he was seeing someone else. Actually that's not true: it wasn't *he* who leaked this critical information. It was Facebook.

Now see, when you find out the man who has been a godlike figure in your life since you were seventeen is now in the arms of someone who isn't you, it tends to wreck your world. Especially when that godlike man coerced you into doing sexual things you weren't ready for while the Catholic community that loved him remained blissfully unaware.

It was easy to stay in a relationship that was destroying me from the inside out because I firmly believed it was the best I'd ever have. In looking for a quick fix to loneliness, I made excuses for his behavior and committed the ultimate sin of romantic relationships: I believed I could *change him.* But I was the one who changed: I went from happy, healthy adult to gradually learning to hate myself, because clearly there was something else wrong with me besides being Jewish (and by most people's standards I wasn't even *that* anymore). There had to be some other reason I was always kept a secret from his family.

Even when I was convinced my family would leave me behind in Israel, I don't think I'd ever felt grief this big. I needed to do a spring-cleaning of my life more than ever, but even that could not be done completely on my own. I hardly ate, slept, or showered within the first week of my newfound "freedom" as an officially single woman. I thought with enough prayer and support from close friends I could get through it, but I couldn't. My mind was a broken record of all the things I should have done sooner, things I wish I'd said. Depression and PTSD taunted me by day and ganged up on me at night.

Eventually, I decided to get counseling so I could at least finish senior year on a strong, healthy note. Sometimes I think it would be easier to forgive John than it would be to forgive myself for staying. But I know there is no point in continually beating myself up. I know that the past cannot be changed or undone.

Jesus' attitude toward forgiveness never struck me as borderline insane until this moment. I had been hurt before, certainly, but never like this. To forgive someone who hurt me this deeply felt ridiculous and unnatural. It contradicted everything I knew to be true about human nature.

By sheer grace alone, I remembered I became a Christian *because* it calls humans to act unnaturally. Christianity calls its followers to rise above their natural inclinations to be mean to people who were mean to us first; it calls us to act on grace instead of revenge. It's the most counter-cultural aspect about Jesus that I'm still trying to understand.

Forgiveness has a bad rap. Some people equate forgiveness with excusing poor behavior, but the reality is that holding on to anger is emotionally crippling (at least for me). It gave John the power to live rent-free inside my head, as the saying goes. He had too much power for far too long, and forgiveness wasn't so much a free pass as much as a choice to keep living.

Still, I struggle with depression every day. Some days are better than others, and then there are days when I wake up and bitterness is the default setting. Some days I cannot pray, because I cannot fathom a god who loves my abuser as much as he claims to love me.

But that's Jesus for you.

22

For Dorothy Gale, a literal whirlwind trip to a place called Oz was enough for her to appreciate the value of Kansas.

A less windy excursion into Christianity was enough for me to appreciate the things I took for granted in Judaism–mainly, the freedom to doubt and ask questions. Christianity isn't anti-doubt and anti-questions, but Judaism, I've discovered, has a more accepting attitude to living with doubts and questions. There's less pressure to have it all figured out, just in case you find someone holding a gun to your head (or threatening to burn you alive), preparing to make you martyr by asking what you believe.

You should only convert once in your lifetime, if you can help it. A person's religion is more than a building to worship in–more than a social gathering, club, or community of like-minded people. Religion influences the way you vote, how you spend your money, how you devote your time, how you view your fellow man, the purpose of life altogether, and the most productive way to live it.

Religion, simply put, is a lifestyle. Ask any convert and I'm quite confident they will tell you: you lose a piece of yourself when you change religions, even if the identity you gain feels like a better fit. Changing religions is like sharing custody of children with your ex-spouse: the interaction may be stiff and uncomfortable, but there is still a bond that can never be severed because of what you shared.

Christians still like to encourage me that I can have it both ways: they tell me I'm a "completed Jew." Such terminology shows how completely uninformed the evangelical culture is at large about Judaism: maybe Christianity *should have been* the fulfillment of the Jewish religion, but that's not how the history plays out. It's irrelevant to me that Jesus didn't intend to create another religion when he started his ministry. Judaism and Christianity evolved in separate directions anyway, and that is the reality we must work with.

It's not enough to convince a Jewish person that Jesus is the real Messiah: the doctrinal differences are so deep, having been developed hundreds of years before the Immaculate Conception. From the beginning, Judaism has viewed the origin of sin, the nature of good and evil, and the importance of the afterlife differently than its brother-from-another-mother, Christianity. Jewish and Christian biblical scholars still battle over how to correctly interpret the original Hebrew manuscripts.

As for me, the former rabbi wannabe, I'm still struggling to interpret the Sermon on the Mount, much less the correct implications of *yom*, meaning "day," and whether it constitutes twenty-four literal hours in the creation story of Genesis, or if Isaiah 53 is prophetically referring to the suffering of Jesus or the suffering of Israel on its beaten path to statehood.

Theology–any theology–is messy, but combining two religions as one is even messier.

I don't claim to be a scholar or an expert in anything. I'm only a pilgrim looking to marry my past to my present in a peaceful way so they don't bicker; a sojourner searching for middle ground between two profoundly different—and profoundly similar— faiths without ending up so infuriated by the followers of both that I toss them both out.

Epilogue

It's been six years since I first prayed to Jesus on the bathroom floor, and I've let go of my childhood desire to be the first Jewish saint. Or any kind of saint, really.

In some ways I feel I've outgrown my fascination with Joan of Arc. She's still my favorite historical figure, but I no longer desire to *be* her. Maybe it's cheesy, but I can only be myself: contradictory, fantastically screwed-up, always curious, still somewhat prodigal, but never boring.

Every single day is a process. Every day is a challenge, some more difficult than others.

If I could do things a little differently, I'd want to have discovered h2o before Cru. Cru is an outreach program, not a church–I understand the difference now. At that fragile point in my life, I was not ready to *know, know, know* the gospel and condense it into an elevator pitch, just in case my paths should cross with an unbeliever (I still don't have that down, in case you're wondering). I didn't have the experience or the knowledge to respond to "purity talks" in the women's groups that lectured females about dressing appropriately so our brothers in Christ wouldn't stumble with lust (because men have no control over their hormones, and women are never visually stimulated. Ever). I didn't know what to say about the "us vs. them" mentality regarding Christians and non-Christians, and the patronizing ways we were taught to evangelize them.

I realize today that there's more to Christianity than evangelicalism, but it's hard to decipher what's true Christianity and what's Christian culture. I think I'm okay living without the latter–many of its precepts are damaging: unhealthy instructions about submission (abusive Christian relationships were never mentioned), sexual education driven by shame for our bodies rather than appreciation for being made in God's image. In time, I also overcame my aversion to the F-word–feminism, that is.

But for what it's worth, my time at Cru was anything but wasted, because I became good friends with one of the guys who helped set up the sound system for the worship band. We're getting married later this year. In fact, we got engaged around the same time as Anne, who will always be "Sister Anne" in my heart, even without the habit.

As far as testimonies go, Joshua and I could not be more opposite: he is a self-described "cradle Christian" who sometimes wishes for a more "exciting" story like mine. I told him to count his blessings; it's not all it's cracked up to be. I wish for more of an "ordinary" testimony like his sometimes. But the testimony thing isn't what matters. You can't change the way you were raised. I'm much more interested in what God is doing in people's lives *right now*.

Time and time again, I've asked myself: what is a Christian? Is it someone who raises their arms high during praise and worship? Someone who prays out loud all the time? Someone who uses a specific set of terms and phrases, like "believer," "quiet time," "guard your heart," and more?

Or is it someone who places their faith in Jesus Christ to pay for their sins; someone who believes his death on the cross was sufficient, that all the good deeds in the world do not earn salvation, and that God loves every human being created in his image?

There are multiple ways of saying it, but I am inclined to choose the latter. My time is best spent among Christians who don't judge me for not doing faith exactly as they do.

My ideal Christian community is not one where everyone agrees on every little thing, but a place where any member is free to express doubts, questions, and personal experiences without condemnation. My ideal church is a place where discussion fuels understanding; where diversity creates respect.

I haven't found that community yet, but I'm working on it.

The more I wrestle with faith, the more I start to believe it's better to be the kind of Christian who admits "I don't know," rather than throwing out the parts of the bible that don't make sense. I really struggled with this when Dad was diagnosed with cancer for the last time, just months before my wedding. I longed to be Jewish again, to return to my roots: I even had the Hebrew word for "life" tattooed on the inside of my wrist–the same symbol Dad always wore on a gold chain around his neck (a gift from his father).

Watching his health rapidly deteriorate, I realized I didn't know for sure what I believed about the afterlife anymore. I also realized there are some things Jews handle better than some churches I've attended recently: things like grieving. Jews, who are no strangers to suffering, don't overly theologize pain. In my experience, Jews don't have the same pressure to reframe it in a more sanitary context, assuring the sufferer that there's a higher, holy purpose for this awful situation. Rather, they accept it for what it is. They aren't afraid to simply say, "That really *sucks*."

I wish more Christians would realize it's perfectly okay to say that sometimes. It's *okay* to not have answers. Sometimes empathizing, not theologizing, is the most Christ-like response.

But I won't go back to my pick-and-choose habits again. I continue pressing on because, as confusing as Christianity can be, I still believe Jesus is a man worth knowing. A man worth living for. He's the original anti slut-shamer: a man who talked to prostitutes, humanizing them while the rest of society would have preferred to have them stoned. He's a man who, after rising from the dead, chose to appear before a woman in a time when a woman's testimony in court was worth the same as a criminal's. He's a man who championed underdogs when he could have had a direct way in to the Pharisees' Cool Table.

He's unique, this Jesus. And God willing, I will continue pursuing him until the end, no matter how difficult it gets.

I believe in a God who embraces all our questions, no matter how difficult. It shows we are serious about seeking him.

Martyrs may be fascinating figures, but they're also extremely rare. They are always there to admire in my books, but I'm more than okay not living like one.

Dear Reader,

The best way for authors to improve their writing is to get feedback. I personally invite you to share your thoughts about this book, good or bad, on Amazon or Goodreads (or both!). Whether you loved it, hated it, or feel somewhere in between, your opinion matters!

-Sarahbeth

Acknowledgements

Amy Jackson, editor extraordinaire: Thank you for consistently turning incoherent streams of babbling into readable books.

Amy Queau: Your beautiful cover designs continue to blow me away.

Kaitlyn Oruska: Expert formatter and best indie friend, it's always a pleasure talking with you.

Finally, to my loving and supportive family: Your love for me has no bounds, and I am insanely grateful for all of you, even when you all drive me bat-nuts crazy.

Excerpt from Sarahbeth Caplin's *Public Displays of Convention*: A romantic comedy inspired by *Pride and Prejudice*

Chapter 1

Today marks the beginning of my New Normal.

Today, my worst nightmare is confirmed. The bottom half of my world drops instantly after reading the following message, barely an hour old on my phone: "Just wanted to tell you I'm seeing someone else now. Still care about you, though. Jared."

I stare at the message for a full ten minutes, thinking over and over, *is this real?* Our conversation from the previous afternoon is still fresh in my mind. If he cares about me as much as he claims to, how could he not have told me about this *then*? How could he drop this revelation on me in such a flippant, undignified way? The humiliation of this–the lack of an honorable face-to-face explanation–is more painful than the breakup itself. Anger simmers in my gut; boils into my lungs. Four years, wasted. *My entire college experience.*

It's late, but sleep is completely out of the question tonight, and there's only one person to call.

"Tess?" I say when she answers. "Can I come over? I–I need to talk."

In best-friend-speak, this clearly means "I'm in the middle of an emergency." Never mind that it's barely been a few hours since we last saw each other. I feel terrible for imposing like this, but am not surprised when she says, "Of course you can, honey. You can even stay over if you want."

She's a godsend, Tess Olsen–my best friend since fourth grade, and the only person I know who talks about Jesus the way most people talk about their crushes. Under her photo in our senior yearbook, where students shared their career goals, all she wrote was her ambition to become a "Proverbs 31 Woman," with a husband and football team of children. She still has a box of letters to her future husband underneath her bed, per our teenage youth group assignment. I did that too for a while, but then gave up because...well, I had Jared.

As her devotion deepened with age, mine

seemed to waver, but she's never judged or condemned me for it. So, somehow, our friendship still works.

I can't stop shaking as I pack my school bag with some overnight necessities and a change of clothes. With uneven breath, I dive straight into snowy oblivion.

Tess' apartment would only be a five-minute walk in normal weather, but the thick wall of snow–unusual for the end of March–makes each step heavy, and I'm a little disoriented with the wind whipping brutally at my face. Still, adrenaline keeps me trudging on.

As tears begin to freeze on my cheeks, only one thought repeats: *Why couldn't I be the one to move on first?* It sounds shamefully petty, but it's devastatingly true. I knew Jared could never be "The One," but I clung to him anyway, thinking it was such an honor to be chosen by a visually stunning, impossibly charming, seemingly genuine man like him. Yet, there was never a time I felt secure enough to believe I was good enough; the thought of being cast off for a woman who could match his allures was always imminent. What a self-fulfilling prophecy *that* was.

Finally, I see Tess through the glass windows of her apartment lobby, and that's when I officially lose it. Once inside her apartment, she places a box of Kleenex and a glass of water in front of me on the kitchen table, and waits for the story to begin.

Once I start talking, the words come out in such a sloppy, tangled mess. I'm amazed she can comprehend any of it. She knows the basic story: how we met at the party of a mutual friend early in my freshman year. I was barely legal; he had just turned twenty-one, and it was love (infatuation? lust?) immediately after "Nice to meet you."

But there is much that she doesn't know; much I made sure she'd never know: the way he'd tell me my opinions were ridiculous; my clothes were either too loose or too tight, revealing too much of a tempting figure, or too much of a too-fat one. The way he refused to introduce me to his other friends, or tell me anything about his family.

I expect Tess to be angry for withholding all this from her. For a while she'd had inklings that something "wasn't right," but I was so careful about keeping his dark side a secret, I don't think she had enough evidence to stage an intervention with me. By the time I finish speaking, she looks very near tears herself.

"I feel so worthless," I whisper.

She shakes her head. "If only you could see

what I see, Anna-Kate" she whispers back. Like a child I lay my head against her shoulder, tears still gushing. I can't believe it's happening like this. I knew the end had to happen sometime, and soon–but not like this. I always thought I would handle it with tact and grace. This is just pathetic.

"Does anyone else know about this?" Tess asks.

I don't quite know how to answer without sounding like a fool. There were other friends, like Carrie and Liv, who knew bits and pieces of this anti-love story as it tragically unfolded, but not any more than Tess knows. I rarely talk to Carrie since she transferred schools, and I stopped mentioning Jared to Liv when, sensing my love for him was greater than his ever was for me, she told me "You're such a smart girl, AK. But you're acting really dumb right now."

Actually, that comment was enough for me to distance myself from her entirely. Now I realize how true it was, but it wasn't what I wanted to hear.

I shake my head at Tess to say "No."

"I know you're feeling worthless right now," she says. "But your worth does not depend on him. Please believe that."

I want to. I really, really want to. But Liv was right–I was a smart girl acting very, very stupid. Every date, every kiss with a man I knew all along was not "The One" was all to feel a little less lonely, a little more secure. And it worked for nearly four years, most of the time. I disgusted myself then; I'm more disgusted now.

CHAPTER 2

I crashed on Tess' couch that night. After only three hours of sleep, I considered skipping my morning class, if only there wasn't a quiz.

My day is miserable. I wander absent-mindedly through campus, ducking into every restroom I pass when I can't maintain a straight face. I wish I could be the kind of woman who may be going through hell, but is able to put on a façade of complacency so no one suspects a thing. But there is no way I can ever be that person.

Back at Tess' apartment, she has prepared an evening of sappy chick flicks and not one, but *two* cartons of Ben and Jerry's. I wear my designated "fat pants" for this night of unabashedly consuming my feelings. I also haven't showered in two days, so now I know I look as gross on the outside as I feel on the inside.

Nonetheless, I'm surprised I can actually laugh at the movie we're watching. Tess' roommate brings over a small group of friends later that evening, and I am instantly embarrassed. Had I known that more people would be coming, I would have made more of an effort to look somewhat presentable. I think, judging by some of the sympathetic looks I got when they arrived, they were able to see that something wasn't right. Thankfully, no one asked or said anything to me.

When the movie ends, I'm still stuffing my face with Doritos, which Tess has to forcefully pry from me–"Enough, Anna-Kate!" She then has to literally pull me up off the couch. "You and I have something we need to do."

"I can't move," I tell her. "I think I gained ten pounds in the last two hours." Surprisingly, the other guests laugh, though somewhat cautiously.

"Glad to see your sense of humor is back," quips Tess. "Now *up*!"

Reluctantly I stand, and a pile of crumbs falls from my lap (which I promise to clean up later). We leave our friends in the living and go to Tess' room, where she closes the door and pulls out her laptop. "You ready for this?" she asks as it boots up.

"No, but what choice do I have?" Sitting on the floor, I draw my knees up to my chest, trying in vain not to let the tears start up again.

"Do you want me to do it?" she asks gently.

"Please."

The most I do is log in to my Facebook account, praying Jared is not online and hasn't left me any messages that will cause me to lose my nerve–but somehow I don't think Tess will allow that to happen. Once that's done–no messages waiting in my inbox–the rest is up to her, and I turn away so as not to catch any unwanted glimpses of recently uploaded pictures of this new woman of his. With just a few clicks, Tess has ceremoniously removed him from my friend's list, and un-sarcastically tells me "All done. I'm proud of you."

"I didn't exactly do anything," I lament.

"Well, you provided your account information, so if nothing else, that makes you an enabler of long-anticipated closure."

"Long-anticipated" is an understatement. Breaking up with Jared should have been done years ago. But I decide against contacting him by other means to speak my final piece; some kind of well-scripted monologue about how I'll be a better woman without him, after which I saunter off with unmistakable confidence. That's not the woman I feel like right now. I doubt I could even *pretend* to pull it off.

It helps to have friends like Tess – friends who aren't afraid to tell you that the man you loved for four years really was a scumbag; that the woman he's with now is probably a ditzy airhead blonde with a ditzy, airhead name like

Candy, who never graduated college and works part-time at a tanning salon. It helps to be told that the man I used to love has probably damned himself to a lifetime of grief with this new woman: a woman with low-enough scruples to trap him into a relationship by getting knocked-up, accidentally-on-purpose.

It's nice to have friends like Tess, who draw up these ridiculous stories to make you feel better, even if you think the real reason the love of your life left you is because you weren't good enough.

CHAPTER 3

After two weeks of sulking, I resolve to start positive today. I think I cried more during those two weeks than I did in the last *year*. At first it felt good to let out that pent-up, overdue grief, but after a while my body ached, and I actually began to crave productivity.

Or at least I thought I did. I made the mistake of checking my email before class this morning, something I don't usually do because it ends up making me late. My heart leapt into my throat when I saw a new message from Jared, and without Tess there to hold me accountable, I knew I wouldn't have the strength to delete it without reading it.

My day had barely started, but these words have now been seared into my mind: "You're just going to act like a child and delete me from your life, is that how it's going to be?" I can't imagine what more he has to gain by keeping me around. He has someone else now, what does he *need* me for? Does he really think I'll be fine with simply being "friends"? Or, more likely, does he enjoy the hold he knows he still has over me?

I won't respond to his message now, if at all. Not when my emotions are all stirred up again. Turning off my computer, I grab my bag and head to class, but at the end of the lecture, I barely remember any of it. I'm angry all over again; just when I thought the worst part of the grieving had passed.

This is how I know just how deeply I am wounded: after changing into sweatpants and an old T-shirt, I walk briskly toward the campus track and start jogging. I *hate* jogging; Jared knew this. The only thing that can propel me to move faster than speed walking is someone chasing me with a sharp object.

I probably look like a crazed idiot, but adrenaline compels me to keep pounding against the pavement, not caring who sees. I imagine fleeing from every dark moment with Jared that made me question my worth, and I imagine that I'm running him over.

Actually, I *do* succeed in running someone over. It must not be a great idea to run when your heart is splintering, when all you see in front of you is pure red. The unexpected thud of my face meeting someone else's chest happens so suddenly, we both collapse on the ground in an ungraceful heap. Wind bursts out of my lungs so painfully I can't respond for several minutes when a male voice asks, *"Are you okay?"*

Completely embarrassed, I fervently nod yes. "I–I'm all right. Just a…a little shocked."

How sad that this man should know I'm a terrible liar before even knowing my name. "You don't look all right. You look upset."

His concern is not unwarranted, but it irks me anyway. "I'm just not used to jogging."

"Yeah, well I'm not used to running into pretty girls who look like they're about to implode. What's your name?"

Did he just call me pretty? "I'm Anna-Kate."

"Nice to meet you, Anna. I'm Collin."

I sigh heavily, having to correct someone yet again for not understanding my double-barreled first name, the bane of my miserable existence. "No, it's Anna-*Kate*. It's hyphenated."

"Ahh, one of *those* girls. Okay, Anna-Kate. Is it okay if I call you AK? No, wait." A menacing twinkle sparkles in his eyes. "I think I'll call you AK-47 for the way you clobbered me."

On a better day, under completely different circumstances, I might have found this amusing. But not today. "Umm, yeah, whatever." Not like it matters. After this confrontation, the most awkward, literal confrontation of my life, it doesn't matter what he calls me since I'm highly unlikely to ever see him again.

Reluctantly, I allow Collin to help me up.

"Shoot straight next time," he says, and with a strange wink he proceeds to sprint away, leaving me to hobble on a scraped knee back to my dorm. I hope I never run into–I mean, see him, again. It's a decent-sized campus, so I suppose the odds of that are in my favor.

After I've showered and made myself a cup of tea, I sit down to tackle Jared's email. After careful consideration, I type, "We both know that what we had wasn't healthy, and I need to get over you. So if you love me like you say you do, please just leave me alone." Without any hesitation, I click the "send" button. Still, I wonder now if I said too much, or perhaps not enough to accurately convey the hurt I feel. As furious as I am, I don't want to appear scathing or vindictive. I can't let him think that I'll wither into a bitter, shriveled excuse for a woman because I don't have him anymore. I should be done caring what he thinks.

Perhaps I should have been clearer that this separation is meant to be permanent. I should have left no doubt that he is not welcome in my life anymore, with or without a new girlfriend in the picture. But even if he tries to crawl back into my good graces, hopefully by then I will reach a point where the thought of taking him back is not the slightest bit tempting.

CHAPTER 4

Spring-cleaning has come early this year. It felt so liberating to take down all the pictures, delete all the emails, and erase Jared's contact information from my phone. However, there are still the contents of my "memento box" to deal with. Much more personal than photographs and text messages, this is a box that contains artifacts from every person who has ever meant something special to me: birthday and Christmas cards from Tess, the collar that belonged to my first pet, even the ticket stub from the movie I saw with my first boyfriend back in ninth grade.

The majority of the contents in this box actually aren't from Jared, but there are enough birthday cards and pictures of him to keep me away for now. I don't trust myself to throw those things away without reliving the way I felt when I first received them. Doing so would crush me all over again, even though he's been nothing like the person who sent them for a long, long time.

After another tiring day of class, I come back to the dorm with the intent of going to bed early. My plans are thwarted by an unexpected distraction: Collin is in the lounge, talking to a guy who lives down the hall. To say I'm shocked is quite an understatement. I wait in the stairwell for a few minutes, but it doesn't seem like he's leaving any time soon. There is no choice but to walk briskly past him, and pray I'm not recognized.

Just when I think I sneaked by unnoticed, I hear him call out "Hey, AK-47! What are you doing here?"

I grit my teeth and stiffly reply, "I *live* here."

"Oh yeah? Well I live here too, three floors up! I was just visiting my buddy Eric here."

The guy I presume to be Eric stands up, informing Collin he's stepping outside for a smoke. How convenient. Once he leaves, it's just the two of us alone in the lounge. I can't explain how or why, but I think I'm starting to smell trouble.

"Nice pin" Collin tells me, pointing to the mockingjay on my bag. "Big *Hunger Games* fan, huh? That's cute."

I'm about to defend my strong devotion to the series, but decide against it at the last second. Now that we are out of the cold, he's wearing a short-sleeved T-shirt. "Says the guy with *Lion King* characters tattooed on his arm," I retort.

"Well I'll have you know that *Lion King* was

the last movie I got to watch with my grandpa before he died. Mufasa reminds me of him."

Holy crap. "I...wow, I don't know what to say. I'm so sorry–"

"*Psyche*! My grandpa is still alive. I just wanted to see your reaction."

"You're an ass-hat."

"Aww, come on now. Can you at least admit I'm a *cute* ass-hat?"

"Well," I stumble. "I guess, since you said my pin was cute…"

Wait wait wait–am I *flirting* with this guy? Someone I only met two days ago? And is *he* flirting with *me*? What am I *doing*?

It's quite shameless, open flirting. There is no way to deny otherwise. I am completely without excuse, other than having my heart blasted to smithereens by the man I loved for the last four years, rendering me temporarily senseless. I'm not the sort of girl who goes looking for rebounds, but I can't stop myself from feeling oddly flattered by Collin's unexpected attention. Dangerously, dangerously flattered.

Having stood up and moved closer to me during this exchange, I realize Collin is close enough to kiss me. Something in his manner tells me if I were to look up at him the right way, it could happen. If I were truly calculating and shameless, I could play this so we end up not only making out, but going back to his room or mine, for God knows what.

With a clearer mind now than when we first met, I notice he is attractive, in a nerdy sort of way. The giant Mufasa tattoo on his bicep is kind of a turn-off, simply because it's too big for my taste; the thought of what that will look like in twenty years makes me cringe. This banter has been amusing, but something in my gut is telling me Collin is more of a charmer than a serious dater. I don't need any charmers right now.

Clearing my throat, I tell him "We should go to bed." His eyes widen, and I instantly realize my idiot mistake. "Go to bed *separately*," I clarify. "It's almost ten o'clock." Good grief, could I sound dumber if I *tried*?

"Right, right," he replies, laughing. Honestly, I don't get the impression that he would have objected if I meant what I'd originally said.

Reaching out with both hands, he holds my arms like he's about to pull me toward him. My breath quickens, and I keep my gaze focused on the floor so there's no temptation to kiss him. Before I can say anything else, he folds me into a quick hug that *almost* turns me to Jello. He breaks away just as quickly with an abrupt "Goodnight!" and disappears down the hall, toward the elevator. I do the same, to *my* end of the hall, not allowing myself to think too deeply on what just happened, or could have happened.

Other books by Sarahbeth Caplin:

Someone You Already Know

Public Displays of Convention

Sorting Myself: a collection of poetry

Where There's Smoke

Made in the USA
San Bernardino, CA
04 January 2015